Master Key
to Self-Realization

Shri Sadguru Siddharameshwar Maharaj

Master Key to Self-Realization

The Spiritual Science of Self-Knowledge
As Presented by Shri Siddharameshwar Maharaj

A Sadguru Publishing Publication

SADGURU

© 2023 Sadguru Publishing

2023, First International Edition

ISBN: 978-1-7376607-2-9

No part of this book may be reproduced or utilized in any form or by any means, electronic or mechanical for commercial or social media usage without written permission from Sadguru Publishing.

Contact Information:
Email:
sadguru.publishing
@gmail.com

Editor and Publisher

This International Edition was previously published in a different form and is a derivative work printed with permission from and in cooperation with Shri Sadguru Trust
Mumbai, India

This book is dedicated to
Shri Sadguru Siddharameshwar Maharaj,
Shri Ranjit Maharaj, and Shri Nisargadatta Maharaj,
as well as their devotees, who in offering
the sweet dish of their devotion, have brought
about the manifestation of this text.

SADGURU

Preface

In this book the reader will find the Master Key to Self-Realization that is in the form of the methodical teaching of Shri Siddharameshwar Maharaj about Self-Knowledge and realization of Final Reality. The teaching contained in this text reflects the clear and direct language that was used by Shri Siddharameshwar Maharaj and that has been similarly used for expressing Advaita Vedanta teachings that have been passed down through the ages. The spiritual instruction contained in this book forms the foundation for understanding the Advaita teachings of Shri Ranjit Maharaj and Shri Nisargadatta Maharaj, and is consistent with the teachings of other great Masters such as Shri Ramana Maharshi, Shri Adi Shankaracharya, and Saint Shri Samartha Ramdas, among others.

Shri Siddharameshwar Maharaj had many Self-Realized disciples. This book was originally written in the Marathi language by Shri Dattatray Dharmayya Poredi a distinguished disciple of Shri Siddharameshwar Maharaj. Upon humble request from several of his disciples, Maharaj narrated the simplified instruction for Self-Realization for the benefit of aspirants which was written down by Mr. Poredi as it was being spoken. Upon completion, he received confirmation of its correctness from Maharaj as well as a pat on the back for a job well done The first Marathi edition of this book was called *Adhyatma Jnanachi Gurukilli* and was published by Shri Ganapatrao Maharaj of Kannur (a brother disciple of Shri Ranjit Maharaj and Shri Nisargadatta Maharaj). This text was studied thoroughly by disciples of Siddharameshwar Maharaj. Many years later, Shri Ranjit Maharaj then received verbal permission from Ganapatrao Maharaj to have the text translated into English. Ranjit Maharaj entrusted the translation responsibilities to Dr. Mrs. Damyanti Dungaji. The completed English translation was then proofread and subsequently published by Ranjit Maharaj. When all of the copies of that original English text were sold, the text was incorporated into another book of Siddharameshwar Maharaj's talks entitled *Amrut Laya*. More recently this has been included in the book named *Master of Self-Realization* written by Shri Nisargadatta Maharaj.

Shri Siddharameshwar Maharaj was the disciple of Shri Bhauseheb Maharaj who mainly taught the path of Meditation as a means to realization. During his spiritual practice, Siddharameshwar Maharaj spent much of his time practicing meditation and reflecting on the teachings of great Saints such as Shri Samartha Ramdas, a renowned Maharashtran Saint of the 17th century (author of *Dasbodh* and *Manache Shlok*), as well as the teachings of Adi Shankaracharya, Valmiki and Vasishtha, and other great Saints such as Kabir, Tukaram, Eknath, (author of *Eknathi Bhagwat)*, and others. After the passing away of his master Shri Bhausaheb Maharaj in the year 1914, Siddharameshwar Maharaj continued meditating on the teachings of his Master. In 1918, he renounced the world and joined four of his brother disciples to popularize his Master's teachings. In the year 1920 when he was on the tour of popularizing his Master's teachings, he got the idea that one could go beyond the path of many years of long meditation as a means for realization and that meditation is an initial stage to attain Final Reality. His brother disciples disagreed with Shri Siddharameshwar Maharaj, saying that their master, Shri Bhausaheb Maharaj has not told them this. He agreed with them, but stated, "Okay! Can one not go beyond that?" He left his co-disciples and returned to his home in Bijapur. While in Bijapur he meditated for nine months continuously without a break. Since his Master had taught him only meditation, he had no other means to find out the way to attain the Final Reality without long arduous meditation. He said, "I will attain the Final Reality even at the cost of my life." By the grace of his Master Shri Bhausaheb Maharaj he attained the realization of Final Reality.

After his realization, Shri Siddharameshwar Maharaj began teaching that in addition to the path of long arduous meditation which is often referred to as "The Ant's Way," one can attain Final Reality very quickly through the path of "The Bird's Way," which is the path primarily of listening to the teachings of the Sadguru, as well as utilizing the power of discrimination (Viveka), combined with thoughtfulness and investigation into one's True Nature (Vichara). This is the most direct path to realization. He said that it is through thinking that Ignorance has become firmly established in one's Consciousness, and it is through thinking that Ignorance can be completely dispelled. His instruction as to how this is done is explained thoroughly within the contents of this text. Truly fortunate are those who come across these teachings in their lifetime. It is the voice of the Supreme Self, Paramatman that is found here in these pages. May the one reading these words attain the realization of the Final Reality with the aid of this text by the Grace of the Sadguru, who is your own True Self.

Jai Sadguru Parabrahman

Table of Contents

Chapter 1: The Importance of Self-Knowledge 1

Chapter 2: Investigation of the Four Bodies - In Search of "I" 21
    THE FIRST BODY - THE PHYSICAL GROSS BODY 24
    THE SECOND BODY - THE SUBTLE BODY 31
    THE THIRD BODY - THE CAUSAL BODY 36
    THE FOURTH BODY - THE GREAT-CAUSAL BODY (TURYA) 37
    BRAHMAN 38

Chapter 3: Investigation of the Four Bodies in Detail 39
    A METHODICAL APPROACH TO EXPLANATION 39
    THE INVESTIGATION COMMENCES 44

Chapter 4: The Great-Causal Body - "I Am" 64

Chapter 5: The Appearance of the World 69
    EXPERIENCING THE CASTES IN A HUMAN BEING 73
    THE THREE WORLDS 75
    UNDERSTANDING THE KNOWLEDGE OF SELF 77

Chapter 6: Maya and Brahman 82
    SEARCH FOR THE LOST "I" 86

Chapter 7: Devotion and Devotion After Liberation 89

Master Key to Self-Realization

Chapter 1: The Importance of Self-Knowledge

At the beginning of this exposition reverential adoration is offered to Shri Ganesh first, then to Shri Saraswati, and finally to Shri Sadguru. What is the reason for offering salutations in this order? If someone were to ask, "If the sequence of this adoration is changed will there be confusion?" The answer has to be, "Yes, there will be confusion." This is because Shri Ganesh is the deity for meditation and contemplation, and Shri Saraswati is the deity for the exposition of the teaching through words. With the help of these two deities, the deity in the form of "The Light of the Self," that arises in the heart of the aspirant, is none other than the Sadguru. Therefore, the Sadguru necessarily has to be adored after Shri Ganesh and Shri Saraswati. Only when the understanding of the subject becomes firm does "The Grace of the Sadguru" descend. Neither the exposition of this text, nor the contemplation on the contents of this text will by themselves lead the aspirant to the goal. Therefore, one should reverentially adore *both* Shri Ganesh and Shri Saraswati.

There is an ancient method of expounding the teaching of Vedanta that is commonly followed in this tradition (Sampradaya) when presenting the subject matter of this text to the aspirant. According to this method, first the manifest form of the Sadguru is seen by the eyes. Then the knowledge about the teachings of the Vedanta, and value and significance of these precious teachings is extolled through the words of the Guru. Then, a Mantra (a subtle name of God, or a phrase) is given and the aspirant is instructed to practice meditation on the repetition of the Mantra for a short period of time (usually several weeks) to imprint its significance within. This provides a means for the aspirant to make the mind more subtle so that the teachings to follow can be more easily grasped and realized. This is the seekers initiation to the teaching and invitation to become an aspirant on the path to realization.

In accordance with the method of the Saints that has been outlined above, the Sadguru first explains about the subject that is to follow, then indicates its characteristics, and finally follows by imparting a detailed knowledge of the subject. In most schools of education, when teaching small children about any subject, the teacher first verbally informs the child about the subject matter that will be taught. This is called the kindergarten method of education. Similarly, initially the Sadguru verbally gives you a concept, or idea of Reality (such as "You are He" or "Only Brahman Exists," or some other similar form of mantra) that is to be contemplated upon. Through repetition or churning, this idea will be indelibly imprinted on the mind. This is called "The Tradition (Sampradaya) of the Sadguru." Through this preliminary method the aspirant achieves results sooner. So be it.

Afterwards, the Guru expounds the Truth (the subject matter) to an ordinarily intelligent aspirant, and he understands what the Sadguru conveys, and about "That" which He is teaching. However, the main difficulty is in experientially realizing what has been intellectually understood. Through the exposition of the subject by the Sadguru, one understands what the Self (Atman) is. However, the ghost of doubt pops up in the mind of the aspirant in the form of the question "How am I the Self?" and the aspirant's mental attitude does not become free of doubt. There is an intellectual understanding, but no realization. The remedy for this is to study with determination, and learn the teaching. Unless there is sustained and repeated study, it will not be fully understood and realized. For example, in the instructional handwriting book, the letters presented are very beautiful. We understand this, but initially we cannot write the letters in the same way. If however the same letters are written repeatedly, then by virtue of that practice or study, the letters are beautifully formed as soon as the pen touches the paper. Here someone might ask, "How much study or practice is required to learn the subject well?" The answer is, "The study, and the practice, or effort must continue relentlessly according to each one's capacity, until it is understood or realized."

A general example can be stated here to impress upon the mind of the aspirant the importance of repeated study. An ordinarily intelligent man can understand something if it is explained to him two or three times. If he repeats it ten or twenty times, it becomes a habit. If he repeats it a hundred times, it becomes like an addiction. Once he becomes familiar with it a thousand times, it becomes inherent nature for the one practicing it. If we look at the fibers of the jute plant, they are so delicate and fine that they become scattered in all directions when blown by the wind. However, when the same fibers are entwined together to form a rope, it is so strong that it can bind even a strong and violent elephant to a small peg. Similarly great is the power of the repetition of the study of this type of practice. It is indeed true that Parabrahman is All-Pervading and Eternally Free. However, the mind in the form of Wind has become so strong in us due to misdirected practice and study through birth after birth that it has imprisoned the eternally free Brahman in the thought of identification with the body. About the tremendous result of repeated practice Saint Tukaram has said, "Whatever is unachievable, becomes achievable only by virtue of repeated study and practice." Recognizing the importance of this study, the aspirant should adore the principles symbolized by Ganesh and Saraswati. This means that he should fulfill himself by continuous meditation, and learn through repeatedly hearing the exposition of Truth.

Now, before one begins this study it will be desirable for the aspirant to know many other things relevant to the subject. Why has the illusion "I am the body" arisen in a human being? What was the condition of the human being when he was born? How did he develop this idea of "me" and "mine"? Is his condition in the world free from fear? If so, by whom and how was he helped to get rid of that fear? All of these things must be taken into consideration.

First, the human being was lying twisted up in a small space inside the mother's womb. When he was born, he came into this boundless world and slightly opened his eyes and looked around.

Upon seeing the immense space and tremendous light, he averted his eyes, and he was in shock. "Where is this that I have come alone? Who is going to give me support? What is going to be my fate?" These types of fear arose in his mind. Immediately after birth, with the first shock, he started to cry. After a little while he was given a drop of honey to lick. With this, he felt relieved thinking that all was well, and that he had someone's support. Thus, he pacified himself. However, that first shock of fear was so ingrained in his mind that he became startled at the slightest sound, and then again becomes quiet when given honey or his mother's breast. In this way, taking external support at every step, this human being became dependent on the support of his parents. As he grew older, his parents as well as those who looked after him as a child started giving him knowledge about the world. After that, his school teachers taught him the various physical sciences such as geography, geometry, geology, etc., which are valueless like dust.

As one enters the stage of youth, he again looks for additional props for his life. As it is determined in the world that support for life comes from money, wife, etc., he gathers wealth and takes on a wife. He takes it for granted that he can be sustained on this worldly support alone, and he squanders away his life. With fame, learning, power and authority, wealth, and wife, he gets added prosperity, and becomes entangled more and more. His principle possessions and his entire support, are his wife, wealth, status, youth, beauty, and authority. Taking special pride in all of this, and becoming intoxicated with worldliness, the human being misses knowing his "Real Nature." The pride about money, pride about authority, and pride about beauty absorb the man and he forgets his Real Nature. Eventually, the above possessions start dwindling one by one. When these possessions start to drop off according to the law of nature, the memory of the original shock that he received earlier shakes him to his very roots, and he becomes frustrated. Panicking, he inquires "What shall I do now? I am losing support from all sides. What will happen to me?" However, this ignorant man does not understand that all these possessions had only one solid support, which was his own Existence, or sense of "I Am." It is by that support alone, that money had its value, that his wife appeared charming, that honor received seemed worthwhile, his learning gave him wisdom, his form acquired beauty, and his authority wielded power. Oh, poor man, you yourself are the support of all the above described wealth! Can there be a greater paradox than to feel that wealth gave you support? In addition to this wealth, power, woman, youth, beauty of form, and honor, if one further receives ill-gotten fortune, how strange and perverted would one's actions become?

A poet once wrote (describing the pranks of the human mind), "It is primarily a monkey, in addition to that he gets drunk, and to top that, a scorpion bites him." Even such a poet would put his pen down seeing the ludicrous absurdities of this human being, and would bid goodbye to his poetic talents. The sort of man who considers his body as God, and is absorbed in its worship day and night should be considered to be like a shoemaker. There is an appropriate proverb that says that a chambar's God should be worshipped only with shoes (in Marathi, the word chambar means "the one who carries a hide on his back"). This tells us the way in which this "God" (the body) of such a man has to be adored. The devotion of an atheist is the feeding of his body, and his liberation is the death of the body. For such a man whose ultimate goal in life is feeding his body, and his liberation is death, there is no rising above the "Gross Body" level. This is not surprising in his case. If due to some misfortune, he were to lose all his wealth, he would still borrow money to indulge in his habits of eating, drinking, and enjoying. If creditors were to hound him, he would declare insolvency to be rid of the whole issue. When death strikes him, ultimately he just lies dead. He passes away just as he had come. Could there be anything more tragic or wretched than this sort of life?

Why should the woman who showers praise on her husband for getting her a lovely nose ring think of the Lord who has provided her with a nose to put the nose ring on? In the same way, how can the animalistic human beings who only look to the body as the "be-all" and "end-all" of life, see God? The One whose power gives the Sun its existence as the Sun, the Moon its existence as the Moon, the Gods their existence as Gods, is the One Almighty God. It is He, who is the support of all, who is present in the hearts of all beings, and has become invisible to man. The one whose eyes are trained on external objects sees only that which is external. The word "Aksha" is a synonym for "eye" in Marathi. "A" is the very first letter of the alphabet, and "ksha" is one of the last consonants. It means that whatever the eye sees will lie within the range of these two letters of the alphabet. It will only bring information or knowledge of external objects. Gross objects will be visualized by the gross eye, and the subtle will be sensed by the senses, which are subtle. However, one letter of the alphabet that comes after 'ksha' in Marathi is "gnya." The letter "'gnya" indicates Knowledge that cannot be seen either by the gross external eye, or the subtle eye of the intellect. Therefore, the intellect and the senses together indicate the "eye" with the synonym "aksha." Like the eye, the other sense organs, the ear, nose, and tongue, are all pointing outwards, and continue to exist on the strength of external objects.

The "King of Knowledge" ("I Am") influences all of the senses, and seems to grant these senses the "Lordship" over the sense objects. It is because of this externalization that the fact that He is present prior to the senses does not attract anyone's attention. Over many births, the mind and intellect have acquired the habit of only looking outwards. Therefore, to "turn within" has become a very difficult task. This is called "the reverse path" which the Saints follow when they turn in the opposite direction, and behold the mind completely giving up seeing all that is external. Where an ordinary man is asleep, the Saints are awake, and where an ordinary man is awake, the Saints dose off. All beings find themselves awakened to external objects, and have become extremely skillful in this type of awakening. The Saints however, have closed their eyes to external things, and it is the Self, to which other beings are asleep, that keeps the Saints wide awake.

One who gets a million rupees is worried about how to double it the next day. He pushes himself to acquire more and more. However, the Saints warn him, "Turn back, turn back, you may be caught in the whirlpool of Illusion (Maya). This Maya has come in like a full tide, and you might be carried away." The modern technological advances that come to this world with newer and newer innovations, as well as those yet to come, make up a cyclone of "Great Illusion" (Mahamaya). Be certain that you will be held captive by it. Who knows to where the one who is caught by this great cyclone will be carried off? When the Saints see one whose attention is taken up by these modern advances running here and there, struggling in his pursuits, they try their utmost to bring about an awakening of Self-Knowledge in him.

There is a story about when Saint Ramdas and Saint Tukaram met each other while standing on the opposite banks of a river. With a gesture of his hand, Samartha Ramdas asked Saint Tukaram "How much awakening have you brought about among the people?" Saint Tukaram replied with a gesture forming his right hand in a fist and putting the back of it to his lips to indicate that nowhere had he found anybody who cared for awakening to the Self. Then Tukaram Maharaj put the same question back to Samartha Ramdas, who then indicated that there was no one awakening whatsoever. They then continued on their way. Saint Tukaram has said, "How can I describe the obligations of the Saints? They are continuously awakening me." Even though it is true that Saint Tukaram and Samartha Ramdas are no longer with us in bodily form, they have given us all that they wanted to teach in the books **Abhangagatha** and **Dasbodh**. The great wealth that they have handed over to us is the priceless legacy of these books. Whoever makes a claim that he is heir to their legacy will enjoy this priceless inheritance. However, the one who wants this wealth must give up the pride of mundane demonical wealth. In addition, whatever acts that one considers as meritorious, and dear to one's heart, must also be renounced. One must be prepared to take a step on the path that turns inward. These are the conditions for becoming a beneficiary to this legacy.

Man is fully immersed in the pride of his body, his caste, his family, his region, his country, and whatever good or bad is in his nature. All of these various types of pride have possessed him. Until he becomes completely free from these various types of pride, how can he claim to benefit from the legacy of this treasure that the Saints have left behind? Only the one whose heart sincerely relinquishes pride can become the beneficiary of this wealth. There is hope for the man who becomes aware of these various types of pride that he has acquired from birth after birth, which have become his second nature, if he sincerely relinquishes this pride. He need not be frustrated. If a slave is awakened to the knowledge that he is a slave, he instantly starts looking for a way to freedom. A slave who finds joy in his slavery, and makes every effort to continue in that condition, cannot even conceive that a highway to freedom exists, until such time that the knowledge of his slavery dawns on him. Similarly, a lucky man who feels that the ambition of getting ahead of others is actually taking him on a downward path, will get from that day onward a glimpse of the reverse direction shown by the Saints. Slowly, he automatically starts making the effort to step onto a new path.

The various types of pride may not leave one all at once. If the aspirant starts to become completely determined to be aware of the pride that he harbors, and begins to leave them one by one, the infinitely "Merciful Lord" will not fail to give him a helping hand. If one takes pride in vicious or evil acts, this should be counteracted by increasing pride in good acts, thus eradicating all of his bad qualities. The good qualities should be nourished and developed. However, one should not be attached to them, and should slowly begin to abandon the pride arising from good actions. A doubt may arise here that although vices deserve to be left, "Why is it that you tell us to leave good qualities also? After all good qualities are always good." Dear aspirants, although the possession of good qualities in comparison with vices and bad qualities seems to be better with regard to the pursuit of attaining Self Knowledge, the possession of the good qualities which one holds dear to one's heart is really a hundred times worse, and truly needs to be thrown out. Look into this, and see. An aspirant tries to leave his bad qualities on the advice of the Saints because of the sense of shame that is created by society or in one's mind, however, the one who possesses good qualities is always getting praise in the world, and is accordingly full of pride about these good qualities. It is very difficult for one to let go of the pride about good qualities.

The pride regarding negative qualities can be left fairly easily, but it is not so in the case of pride regarding good qualities. Nobody wants to admit that he has committed any error, but the pride that one harbors when he has given meals to thousands who have visited the four holy places, or opened lodging for holy people, or worshipped the deity millions of times, becomes so firm in him that it becomes almost impossible to give up. It is when one recognizes one's worldly ways and is ready to relinquish them that he soon finds a Sadguru. However, the one who is sought after by everyone for performing many good deeds, gets so deeply buried in the flattery that is showered upon him, that his way to the Sadguru becomes lost due to his pride. Realizing this, one must conclude that pride about bad qualities is tolerable, but the pride about good qualities is best to be avoided completely. Both the pride about one's good qualities and pride about one's bad qualities are thorns on the path to Self-Knowledge. When one thorn is pulled out with the help of another thorn, there still remains the second thorn (pride of good actions) that one carries around in the shirt pocket. Will this thorn not also prick the chest or rib? If a thief is shackled by iron handcuffs and a king by golden handcuffs, does that mean that the king is not bound?

Take it for granted that while the man in the iron cuffs will thank someone who frees him from them, the man with the golden cuffs will pounce on the throat of anyone who tries to free him. He will try his best to permanently keep the golden cuff on his hands. What is the force behind this? Who is this "friendly enemy" in this example who makes one feel so happy in his bondage? It is the pride one has in good deeds that is the real archenemy of the aspirant. This pride is the enemy who blocks the way to "Ultimate Truth" (Paramartha). Therefore, it is necessary to renounce any pride that one has about good deeds. This may require tremendous effort, but without renouncing all pride, the aspirant can never claim his legacy to the wealth of "Knowledge." It is believed by many that a man's worldly wealth such as money, a beautiful wife, status, etc. is the result of meritorious deeds done in previous births, but these very beliefs act as boulders obstructing the way to finding the "Ultimate Truth." Therefore, it may be said that these things are really the result of body identification (the definition of sin). When a person is infused with pride, he becomes possessed, and therefore becomes incapable of treading the path of Ultimate Truth.

Contrary to the wealthy man, there might be a man who does not have a penny, who is quite ugly, has no wife, no status, and is so poverty stricken that in order to fill his belly, he is willing to eat whatever food he could get from anyone. He may have lost his caste, family, friends, and all who were dear to him. This homeless wanderer may be naked on all fronts, and even believed to be wretched by the whole society, yet he truly may be more worthy of gaining Self-Knowledge, because he is naturally free of pride. The ears of someone like this poor naked man turn towards the Sadguru sooner than one whose ears are filled with flattery. The one who is puffed up with pride has no room for receiving the advice of the Sadguru. Such a person has no time to turn to the Sadguru's advice even for a minute. The whole of humanity has become entangled in Illusion from birth, and lives in bondage. In addition to this, man creates many types of artificial bondage around him in the form of comforts and attachments resulting from ever newer inventions. If man has to live in modern society, he has to abide and respect the norms of traditional social conventions, and governmental rules. For example, wearing a necktie in order for one to do one's daily work is supposed to be the proper social etiquette. In these types of ways, to be up to date in society makes one feel that he is getting more and more freedom. In modern society, if one does not indulge in drinking or drugs, or does not shave everyday, he is considered a social outcast. By diving into the bondage of such a society and holding such silly ideas dear to the heart, one only continues binding oneself, only further increasing the pride that one has about worthless things. Unless these types of social bondage and pride are completely thrown off, and unless one is considered to be a "madman" by the "socially wise" people, there is no hope that one will arrive at such a mental state that allows one to be free from pride, and such "social bondage." The Sadguru's only aim is to help one to become completely free of all pride, and to eradicate the identification with the body. If the aspirant finds the renunciation of all pride and social bonds difficult to do, or is unwilling to formally renounce his wife, money, or estate, he can begin with inward renunciation. When this becomes successful, the formal renunciation slowly becomes possible.

Inward renunciation means renunciation that is undertaken with the mind. For example, there may be someone who has the habit of hurting others with harsh words. It does not cost the aspirant anything to replace that habit by saying only kind words to others. As another example, there may be some people who have the habit of telling lies unnecessarily, in their case, they should begin renunciation by stopping the telling of lies, at least until such time that an occasion arises where unless they tell a lie, some great calamity may occur. This type of mental renunciation will also not require any expenditure. While looking at a neighbor's prosperity, one should not be envious of his neighbor. Will making such a decision bring the aspirant any harm? In this way, when one begins to renounce negative qualities, he also begins to gain strength in renouncing external things. This world is like a dream, and in this dream-like world whatever is considered to be good or bad, merit or sin, or anything in the realm of dualistic morality is of no consequence in the process of awakening to the Self. Therefore, renunciation of both sides of duality such as good and bad, or auspicious and inauspicious, is necessary to gain Self-Knowledge. Even though this may be understood, it is still difficult to eradicate pride. No matter how often someone may repeat to himself to "renounce, renounce," it will not make even the slightest dent on pride. However, if the reason why this pride enters one is discovered, it can be eradicated, and renunciation automatically follows. The aspirant must come to understand that the reason why one harbors pride for objects is because he believes the objects to be true.

If one understands that objects are only a temporary appearance, and becomes convinced that objects cannot really provide true happiness, then the apparent reality of the objects automatically fades away. It then becomes possible for one to develop detachment for those objects that were previously held dear to one as true. A wooden toy in the shape of a tamarind pod is not a real tamarind pod. It is made of wood. However, unless one has the discriminative ability to be able to tell the difference, the sight of the wooden tamarind is sure to make one's mouth start watering. The reason for this is the conviction that the thing is real. Once one becomes aware that the tamarind is made of wood, he may appreciate the artistic or aesthetic lines of the toy, but it will not affect his salivary glands. This discriminative knowledge, or the recognition that it is not real, results in true detachment towards the object. This example shows us that the detachment towards objects is brought about by understanding their true nature. Unless the futility of acquiring objects in this world is impressed irrevocably upon the mind, Self-Knowledge is difficult to attain. Unless one understands the false nature of objects, one will never aspire for the "Real Thing." There can be no renunciation of the false as long as the intellect believes it to be true. The day that the wrong knowledge regarding the world is eliminated by virtue of the Sadguru's advice, one becomes convinced that this entire world is only a temporary appearance. When this happens, one becomes able to look at the world and appreciate it as if it were a cinema, or a source of entertainment, and with the detachment that has been achieved, one remains unaffected.

Detachment without Self-Knowledge is like what is experienced when one is watching the activities going on at the cremation grounds. Without Self-Knowledge, there can be no real renunciation, and without renunciation, there can be no Self-Knowledge. This is the paradox. The Saints have given us various methods of getting out of this situation through such means as devotion to the Guru and God, singing the praises of the Guru and God (Bhajans), visiting holy places, giving in charity, etc. In this way, the Saints have given an infinite number of means of salvation to humanity. Human nature is such that if a man is forcibly robbed of a thing, he suffers immensely. He will make persistent efforts to regain that thing. Yet, if he were to part with the same thing out of his own free will, that sacrifice would bring him immense joy. A man who is normally unwilling to spend a dime under compulsion, would out of his own free choice spend thousands in order to feed the people at a religious gathering. However, there are countless examples of how after mixing with Saints, and chanting Bhajans, even very proud people have changed. One whose pride previously would not have allowed him to submit to another person's will is now willing to bow in submission to someone even of a much lower standing in society. By his keeping the company of Saints, he naturally and easily completely forgets his pride of caste or social status. That "important man" who was filled with pride, and felt ashamed to even apply sandalwood paste to his forehead in his own house, now allows Buka (a black powder) to be smeared on his face, indicating a total lack of pride. The same person who previously considered singing and dancing obscene, forgets himself and his body, and starts dancing in ecstatic joy with a partner, while chanting the name of God. Understanding how aspirants sacrifice pride in this way, the Saints have given mankind the teachings prescribing Bhajans and Puja (Worship) for daily practice. With this teaching, they have pointed out a progressive step on the path of Self-Knowledge. In this way, they impress upon the aspirant how easy it is to renounce the objects of the world, and how to clear one's mental attitude from pride.

Self-Knowledge is the Knowledge about one's Self. Once we recognize who we really are, then automatically the determination is made regarding what is permanent and what is transient. Then, very naturally the renunciation of the impermanent, and the acceptance of the permanent follows. Because of the transient nature of things, the fear of dissolution is inevitable. The one who is overpowered by this fear of dissolution, or death, continuously strives to see that some particular thing is not taken from him. He takes every precaution to preserve his money, tries hard to see that his wife's youth and beauty does not deteriorate, and struggles to keep his status and authority. However, try as he may, nothing ever happens according to his wishes or desires. No one can escape their destiny, and because death is all-consuming, everything will eventually get crushed in its jaws. Even Gods like Brahma are not free from the fear of death.

Even if such a fear-ridden man were given everything he desired, could he avoid being afraid? If he needs anything at all, it is the gift of fearlessness. The aspirant must find that which will free him from fear permanently. This beggar called man, who has lost his own treasure of the Self, continuously chants "I am the body, I am the body." He is forever discontented saying "I want this, I want that," and wanders around always begging for something in the world. He can only truly be pacified with the gift of the Self. The man who chants "What will happen to me, my wife and children, and the money that I consider to be mine?" is always disturbed and upset. This sort of man needs to be given the gift of fearlessness, and thus be made fearless. Only the Sadguru is generous enough, and capable of bestowing the gift of fearlessness, which is the noblest of all the gifts. Kings and Emperors, and even Gods are incapable of granting this gift of fearlessness. Although all earthly wealth is at the feet of an emperor, he is restless with fear at the very thought of an enemy attack. Even Lord Indra is anxious day and night with the thought that his status as "King of the Gods" might be shaken by the austerities and practices performed by some sage. Think deeply on this. Can those who have not freed themselves of fear give the gift of fearlessness to others? Only those Great Saints, the "Mahatmas," who have uprooted fear from its very depths by establishing themselves in the Self and destroying the identification with the body are capable of granting the gift of fearlessness. Except for these Mahatmas, the hosts of gods, demons, and men are like penniless beggars. They can never get the gift of fearlessness unless they take shelter with a Sadguru. If they are gods, they entertain the pride of godly wealth, if they are demons, they carry the pride of their own vicious wealth on their heads, and human beings are crushed under their own burdens. Gods are no better than servants who carry other people's burdens on their heads. What is the lowly status then of the human beggar? It is only the Sadguru who extends his hand to lift their burden, and blesses them at the same time with the gift of fearlessness.

Out of all the various types of knowledge, Self-Knowledge is the greatest, and of all the paths, or dharmas (dharma is one's religion, or one's nature), Swadharma is the most noble. The Mahatmas spread the "Knowledge of the Self" among men and teach them the meaning of Swadharma. In this world, the knowledge of astrology, black magic, public relations, the fourteen types of sciences, and the sixty-four arts are taught. However, all that knowledge except for "Knowledge of the Self" is false knowledge. Saints refuse to recognize these other types of knowledge, and spread only the "Knowledge of the Self." Many missionaries who are competing with one another assert their opinions and start giving advice saying, "My religion is the noblest, and all others will only lead one to ruin." Not only do they just give advice, but also they fulfill their sacred duty of conversion, sometimes through bribes, or threats of burning people's houses, or sometimes even by killing people. Without much change from days of old, this kind of propagation of religion is going on even today. This piracy of religion full of compulsion and tyranny is not useful for accomplishing the well-being of anyone.

Saint Ramdas said, "If there is any one religion in the world that is noblest of all, it is Swadharma." Swadharma means to live in one's "True Nature." To live in one's innate nature is Swadharma even though one may belong to any caste, religion, or nation. To understand Swadharma, one should realize that it is existent in all forms of life, be it an ant, or an insect. One's "True Nature" alone is Swadharma and all other paths or cults parading as religions are "paradharma," meaning that they are religions pertaining to something that is other than the Self. These various cults and religions put down certain rules and methods which are alien to our real nature. This is how we can define Swadharma and paradharma. If we take for granted the currently accepted meaning of Swadharma (one's inherent nature), it can be considered absurdity. Suppose there is a prostitute. She also has a relevant dharma, her nature, which she follows diligently believing that it is her swadharma, or her true nature, her true religion. She teaches the same to her daughter from the time she is in the cradle, and in the end she dies following her own religion. Who can say, perhaps some "Streetwhore Swami" (a lover of women) may even come forward to include that woman's life story in some book about religious saints.

The Lord has cautioned us in the Bhagavad Gita, "It is best to die in Swadharma (the death of body identification, which brings one into the Self). Dharma that is alien, is full of danger. While trying to achieve this, if death comes, it is to be preferred over following some other dharma which is alien to the Self." The aspirant should recognize the importance of the caution that is being imparted in the translation of the Lord's words. Eradicating the idea of identification with the body is the sign of the "Knowledge of the Self." Mahatmas experience this type of death while living. This type of death is to be preferred over the death that occurs when following someone else's religion. Saint Tukaram said, "I have seen my own death, how shall I describe that process which is unique?" How can those who live in a religion that is not of the Self, and who die a corpse's death, understand this process of death while living? The unfortunate one only thinks of death in terms of various customs and rites according to one's religion. Those dharmas built on the strong basis of body identification contain the dualities of temptation and fear, heaven and hell, merit and sin, and bondage and liberation. Every human being has the right of following Swadharma, his own nature where there is no temptation of heavenly enjoyments and no fear of pain in purgatory, and where bondage and liberation have no meaning. There is a cruel but true maxim that states, "Whatever comes has to go." All of the recent "pseudo-religions" are spreading because of their newness, and in some cases even with government patronization. They will definitely sink to the bottom, and there will be nothing but glory and victory to Swadharma alone. (Note - During Shri Siddharameshwar Maharaj's time, the Government in India was in many cases helping to fund religious schools and even missionaries. In this paragraph all religions that are not of the Self are being called "pseudo-religions," not being of our "True Nature," or "Swadharma," and ultimately they will not last)

Lord Krishna advised Arjuna on this. He said, "Leave aside all religions and come seek refuge in Me. Come to Me, and leave off all of those religions which create hindrances on the path to reaching Me. Seek refuge in Paramatman who is of the nature of Self-Knowledge. You will have realized your Self when you attain Me, and there will be nothing more for you to do. All karma (actions) gets exhausted in Self-Knowledge." On the pretext of advising Arjuna, Lord Krishna has given this advice to all human beings that they should fulfill themselves by accepting this advice that He has given. There is nothing in the whole world as sacred as Self-Knowledge. All other "work" or "action" is meaningless. In this context one should not think that all other types of knowledge or actions except Self-Knowledge are useless, meaning that they are of no value, or without any result. However, they are of no help in achieving Swadharma. It is not that getting results such as a son, or heaven, by means of performing sacrifices is not possible. By studying scriptures, one does become proficient, and it is possible for one to appease various deities by worshipping them. Even if this is so, and even if all these actions are supposed to be meritorious in this mundane world, they are still hindrances as long as the Self is not pleased, and does not shower His Grace. The qualities valued as best in the practical world only count as disqualification, and all remedies only turn into obstacles in pursuit of Self-Knowledge. The sages know this well and do not even care in the slightest if they are able to conquer all of the three worlds. They consider Lord Indra's status, that is ridden with jealousies, to be as useless as the droppings of a crow. The Saints harbor only one desire in their hearts, and that is the desire of achieving "Oneness with Brahman." With regard to everything else, they are desireless. Those Saints who are represented by statues of auspiciousness became one with Brahman when their Consciousness became dis-identified from their body. In ordinary cases, the body is viewed only as a corpse, while in the case of those Mahatmas, they became worthy of worship, and they receive adoration from people. Not only this, but also many temples were built around their shrines. Thus, they became immortal by becoming the object of worship and adoration from the whole world.

Rama, Krishna, Siddhartha, Hanuman, Malhari, Jagadamba, were Mahatmas in the form of Gurus. While they were alive, they did the work of spreading Knowledge and they became Gods when they left the body. All the temples on earth belong to these very Gods who grant the wishes of devotees according to their vows and desires. They lift the aspirant to their own level and bring them to the achievement of Self-fulfillment. Many people think that the God that one worships meets him (when he sees a vision) and gets his work done, but God is not limited to one point or place as the devotee imagines. He resides in the devotee's heart as well as in every heart, and it is He who inspires one to get one's work done. Nobody should ever entertain the wrong idea that after the Mahatma leaves his body, he assumes the same body again and comes out of his Samadhi (comes back from the dead) and then gets his devotee's work done.

When you wish that a certain person should get ten rupees at Pune (a city in Maharashtra State in India), you give a ten rupee note in cash to the main Post Office at Sholapur. On the second or third day, you get the receipt indicating that the intended person has received the amount that you have sent. Have you ever made inquiries to the effect that the same note, or the same coins that you handed over to the Post Office have reached the intended person? No, this type of question never even arises in your mind. Your attention is centered not on that exact note, but on the value of the note. When the amount sent has reached the person, you do not have any complaints. In the same way, these past Saints and Mahatmas who have turned into Gods get the devotees work accomplished through the Mahatmas that are living today, and who are of the same caliber. This is the way their devotees' wishes are fulfilled.

What magical skill did these persons possess who were honored in their lifetime and became immortal, thereby retaining their fame even after their bodily death? What special learning did they have that they should be adored by people even after death? In this world, there are many arts and sciences. Many discoverers and many adventurous heroes are praised during their lifetime. These heroes are congratulated and covered with garlands of flowers, and bouquets. The people even express their admiration for the heroes by carrying them on their shoulders. However, in due time, a hero who had been an object of people's adoration soon becomes a subject of their abuses. Soon people who were pampered as heroes for a few days, are condemned in an assembly. Sometimes, even resolutions condemning them are carried out. It is clear that the greatness of these heroes is artificial and not everlasting because their "greatness" is based on transient learning or adventures. Their greatness is not based on the sacred learning that gives everlasting peace like the "Knowledge of the Self." It is based on some science such as politics with some practical motive. In politics names and faces continue changing with time, and in the physical sciences new discoveries follow one after another. A person who was once proclaimed as great is found to be of no importance and in some other corner of the world some other person starts shining on the horizon. The greatness that is achieved through any learning other than Self-Knowledge eventually takes an opposite direction. Because of this, these "great ones" have to suffer the sweet and sour experiences associated with honor and insult. It is no wonder that no one goes to the trouble of thinking about these "great men" after they are dead.

Out of all the types of Knowledge (Vidya), Self-Knowledge (Atma Vidya) is the only Knowledge that grants everlasting peace. One Saint asked, "What is the use of any knowledge that does not grant peace of mind?" There are many types of courses of learning that are available in the world. Why is there such a proliferation of courses? The reason is that no one has found peace of mind. The struggles in the world have not stopped even a little because the restlessness of the mind has not ceased. Why is this? It is because all of these sciences and arts are centered in Ignorance, and they are useful only for increasing the agitation and restlessness of the human mind. There is no relationship of cause and effect relating learning to peace. The one who evaluates various kinds of gems, and one who examines various sciences and arts, or aesthetics, has lost the happiness that comes from peace of mind because they have no ability to examine themselves.

Why should one search another man's house when he has not searched his own house for something that he lost while he was at home? The man who boldly asserts "This man is like this, and the other man is 'Mr. A' or 'Mr. B,'" while he does not know who he is himself, is never free from restlessness. It would be futile to discover what thing could be extracted from where, or to know many addresses, if one does not know one's own address.

Chapter 2: Investigation of the Four Bodies - In Search of "I"

Who is this "I"? Once upon a time, there lived a man named "Gomaji Ganesh" who lived in a town called Andheri. At one point in time, this man established a custom in the Courts of Law that no order or document could be accepted as legal unless it bore a stamp with his name on it, along with the words **"The Brass Door."** From that point on, all of the officials of that town only accepted a document as being legal if it bore the stamp of **"Gomaji Ganesh, The Brass Door."** This procedure for making documents legal continued for a long time until eventually the stamp officially became part the legal system of the City of Andheri, and no one ever enquired as to just whom this "Gomaji Ganesh" was. As time passed, it happened that one day an important document that did not bear the official stamp of **"Gomaji Ganesh, The Brass Door"** was cited as evidence in a case filed in the Court of Law. Except for the fact that this document did not have the official stamp, it was otherwise completely legal according to all other points of law and ordinary procedure. At one point in the case, an objection was raised that the document should not be accepted as evidence because it did not bear the official stamp of **"Gomaji Ganesh, The Brass Door."**

At that point, a courageous man who was a party to the lawsuit argued before the judge that the document was perfectly valid because it bore all of the relevant signatures of the current government officials. He argued "Why should the document not be admissible if it is otherwise perfectly legal except that it does not bear the stamp of Mr. Gomaji Ganesh? Thus, he questioned the legality of the stamp itself. Consequently, the legality of the stamp was made an issue of contention. Until that day, no one had ventured to bring this issue before a Court of Law. Since it had now arisen for the first time, it was decided that a decision should be made regarding the legality of this stamp. Out of curiosity about how the procedure of the stamp of **"The Brass Door"** came to be put in place, the judge himself took the matter in hand for inquiry. When his inquiry was completed, he discovered that many years in the past, a man of no particular status, a Mr. Gomaji Ganesh, had taken advantage of the badly administered government of his day, and put his own name on a stamp that was to be used for all official documents. From that time onward, all government officials simply continued following the tradition blindly. In fact, the judge discovered that Mr. Gomaji Ganesh was a man of no importance whatsoever, who had no authority of any kind. When the judge made this discovery, a decision was made by the Court that the stamp was no longer necessary for legal documents. Since that day, the stamp was looked upon with ridicule. In the same way, we should inquire about the sense of "I," and how it dominates everything with the stamp of "I," and "mine," just like the stamp of Mr. Gomaji Ganesh described in the above story. It is a general rule or principle in nature that if two things are combined, some new third thing is produced.

For example by the contact of a piece of thread with flowers, a garland is produced that did not previously exist. Even the names of the parent objects whose contact was responsible for producing the garland disappear as soon as the garland comes into existence. The garland then comes to be known by its own label. The labels of "flowers" and "thread" become extinct, and the new name of "garland" is used, and with that new name, further action takes place. With the contact of earth and water, mud arises as the labels "earth" and "water" become extinct. In much the same way, stones, bricks, mud, and mason come together, and a third thing called a "wall" stands before our eyes, while the stones, bricks, mud, and the mason simply vanish from our sight. It is by the coming together of Knowledge and Ignorance that a peculiar thing called the "intellect" comes into existence, and it is through this "intellect" that the contact with the world emerges. Gold and goldsmith come together and produce a third thing that appears before our eyes as an ornament. The ornament is seen, and the gold and the goldsmith are forgotten. As a matter of fact, if anyone was to try to find out if there is any such thing as an "ornament" inside the gold, one would see nothing but gold. If we tell someone to bring an ornament without touching the gold, what could he bring? The thing we call an ornament would simply vanish. In the same way, out of the union of Brahman and Maya (Illusion), the thief called "I" has come along proudly saying "I," and raising its head proclaiming sovereignty over both Brahman and Maya. This "I," or ego, is a barren woman's (Maya's) son, and that one who does not actually exist, tries to establish unlimited sovereignty over the entire universe. If we observe the parents of this "I," it is clear that it is impossible for them to give birth to such a child. The mother of the child is Maya, who does not exist. From the womb of this Maya, the "I" has come forth. It is supposed to have been produced by the "Life-Energy." Yet, this Life-Energy (Brahman) has no gender, and does not even claim to possess "doership," so the readers can imagine what kind of an "I" this is.

As described above, the existence of "I" is only in name. Yet, like Mr. Gomaji Ganesh, he announces his name everywhere as "I." He goes around saying "I am wise, I am great, I am small," all the while having forgotten from where he came. Instead, he starts glorifying himself as "I," like the cat who laps up milk with its eyes closed, not aware of the stick that is ready to strike him from the rear. As soon as he accepts a right, or a privilege, he must also accept the responsibility that goes along with it. As soon as one says, "I am the doer of a certain act," that "I" must enjoy the fruits of such action. Enjoyment and suffering of the fruits or the results of action are tied to the action itself, and to the identification as the doer. Actually, no such thing as an "I" exists. The entire doership that is the motivating force behind the "I" is contained solely in Brahman. However, Brahman is so brilliant, the moment that he finds someone who takes pride in "doership," he leaves all responsibility for the actions on the head of that "I" and remains unattached. Consequently, the poor "I" is destined to revolve on the wheel of birth and death. In the example of the garland mentioned above, the name "garland" came forward after the names "flowers" and "thread" were forgotten. When the garland dries, up nobody says that the flowers have dried up, they say the garland has dried up, or if the thread snaps, they say the garland has snapped. This indicates that the "doership" of the original object is imposed upon the third object due to the pride, or identification with the object. In the same way, a series of miseries strike the non-existent "I." If one wants to get free from this misery, he must leave the "I." However, before it is left off, one has to find out exactly where this "I" resides. It is only when we find the "I," that we can talk about leaving it off. The aspirant should begin the search for this "I" at his or her own center. It will never be found outside of us. In every human being this sense of "I" or ego, and "mine," the feeling of possession, is filling one up to the brim. All the actions in the world are carried out by the force of this ego, and the sense of "mine." The assumption of "I" is taken for granted by all human beings. However, all actions can be carried out without this ego, or the sense of "mine." How this can be done shall be seen later. Presently we will discuss only this sense of "I" and "mine."In order to trace this "I" let us first examine our own Physical Gross Body that seems so close to us. After analyzing it, let us see if this "I" can be found anywhere in this body.

The First Body - The Physical Gross Body

What is a body? It is a collective assembly of parts (limbs and organs) such as hands, feet, mouth, nose, ears, eyes, etc. The assembly of all these parts is called the "body." Out of these various parts, let us find out which one is "I." We can say that the hand is "I," but if the hand is cut off, nobody says "I have been cut off," or "I have been discarded." Suppose the eyes go blind. No one says, "I am gone," or if the stomach is bloated, no one says, "I am inflated." No, instead one says "my hand is cut off," or "my eyes have gone blind," or "my stomach is expanded." All of these parts are spoken of as "mine." Not only that, but the body itself that is an assembly of all these parts, is also spoken of as "my body." By looking in this way, it can easily be seen that the one who asserts ownership of all the limbs, and even of the body itself, is really someone who is quite different from the body that he calls his own.

We have stated above that the "I" is not any part, or any of the limbs of the Gross Body, and that all the limbs are considered as "mine." There is an established general truth, or maxim, that says, "Where the 'I' does not exist, there cannot exist anything that can be called as 'mine'." From this maxim, it follows that the body and limbs actually do not belong to "me," as there is not any "I" residing there. The same maxim applies if "I" do not reside in the neighbor's house, can the neighbor's house, or its contents or associated parts belong to me? If one wants to verify the truth of the maxim "Where there is no I, there can be nothing of mine," one only has to go to a neighbor's house and say "I am master here, and the wife of this household is also mine." If you try to show your sense of "mine" to the wife in that house, and start making advances towards her, you will quickly see what kind of an experience you will get. The true master of the house would hit you so hard that you would quickly realize "I am not the master here, and she is not mine." In the same way, when the "I" cannot be traced anywhere in the body then how can it be said that the limbs of the body and its tendencies belong to "me". If you still insist upon calling it your own, find out why, and also look closely at the condition of all human beings who look upon their bodies as their own and act accordingly.

The human being forgets his True Self, and does not understand who he really is. Therefore, he has to take many births in numerous species. Sometimes he becomes a worm and passes out in a stool. Sometimes he becomes a bullock and gets yoked, turning around and around in a mill. Sometimes he becomes a donkey and works hard wallowing in a heap of garbage. How many such miseries one has to suffer is almost impossible to describe. After suffering births in all the other species, finally one gets the good fortune to be born as a human being. This birth in the human body is unique as it has the capacity for higher intellect and discrimination so that we can know God, the "Supreme Self." If we look at the body of the human species, it can be compared to a dressed-up character in a vulgar play during the period of the *Shimga* festival. This character can be described thus: The character's face is smeared with black paint, the body is dressed up in rags with a garland of shoes around his neck, and an umbrella made of shoes is held over his head. Then, this character is seated on a donkey and taken in a procession through the streets accompanied by various strange noises. Ironically, this character takes pride in being the center of such a demeaning show, and salutes people on the street. In the same way, one's body is also a peculiar part of this passing show. All the beauty of the face is supposed to be concentrated in the nose and eyes. We say that a man is handsome or a woman is beautiful if they have a good nose and good eyes. However, what is the nose except a tube for nasal discharge?

The mouth is like a spittoon full of saliva and phlegm. The stomach resembles a sewage plant of some city. The body is given some respectable name, but it is only an accumulation of bones, flesh, and blood. It is the intention of the Supreme Self, to awaken the human being by demeaning him and making him miserable with the body. He then makes the human being cry aloud for happiness, and wander about in all directions in search of it. In spite of this, the human being considers the body to be great gift, and with joy he describes it with flowery language. The nose, which is a tube of mucus, is compared to the bud of some beautiful flower. The eyes, which are the places of abundant discharge are called lotus eyes. The face, with a mouth like a spittoon full of saliva, is called a moon face, and the arms and legs which are like crooked branches of a tree, are referred to as lotus hands and lotus feet! The human being looks upon this type of behavior as normal, and exhibits his foolishness shamelessly.

However, the Great Lord grants a wonderful thing called the "higher intellect" even to this "Shimga" character of a human being that He has not given to any other species. The purpose of that gift of higher intellect is for the human being to be able to realize the "Divine Nature of the Self" and put an end to this demeaning show. However, the human being misuses this great gift of the intellect. He looks upon a gutter as the Ganges, and the body as God, and only spoils it further. The human being spends a lot of his time adorning the Physical Body. Taking this body as "I," he then comes into contact with a female body and begins calling that person as his own. He then begins to place the sense of "mine" or possession on that female body. By virtue of the contact of this "I," with that which is "mine," many children are born and a whole household is brought into existence. The household eventually gets shattered, and the poor man suffers ridicule. This story has been described in great detail in the book *Dasbodh* by Shri Samartha Ramdas. It is strongly recommended that this book be studied and thoroughly understood.

We have determined that the "I" cannot be traced anywhere in the body. It is also a fact that the body is not "mine." Then to whom does the body belong? Who is the "owner" of the body? The five elements (Earth, Water, Light (Fire), Air (Wind), and Space) have the right of ownership to this body. After the body falls, each of these elements takes away their own share, thereby destroying the body. The body is a bundle of these five elements. By analogy, it's like clothes that were tied up in a bundle and have now been taken away by their respective owners, and even the cloth in which the bundle was wrapped up has also been taken away. How then, can anything called a "bundle" remain? There is not even anything left that can be seen.

In the same way, once the body that is composed of the five elements is unbundled and dispersed back into those five respective elements, there remains no object such as the body. Examining in this way, we can see that "I" am not in the body, nor does the body belong to me. This type of body consisting of a bundle of the five elements cannot support any pride of "I" or an "ego." Nor can it sustain the relationships that existed due to the identification with the body, such as birth and death, or the six passions (greed, anger, desire, hatred, craving, and pride) that affect the body. These cannot be related to any "me," as being "mine." The body may be in a state of childhood, or youth, or old age, or the body may be dark, fair, beautiful, or ugly. It may be infested with disease, it may be just wandering aimlessly, or going to holy places for pilgrimages, or it may be motionless in samadhi. All of these attitudes, properties, and modifications belong to the body, but the "I" is separate from all of these.

From the analysis of the Physical Body, we have learned that the "I" is separate from all of its qualities. Additionally we can easily see that someone else's beautiful cute bonnie baby is of no value to us, compared to our own dark stocky boy who has pockmarks, and who has a flowing dirty nose. We do not suffer if someone else's sweet child dies as much as we suffer if our worn old shoe gets lost. The reason for this is that we do not have the same sense of "possession" or "mine" for the other person. Once one understands that some particular thing is not "mine," and that it belongs to someone else, he becomes indifferent about that thing. He even gradually starts disliking that thing which belongs to "someone else," or "another," and then it is easily renounced. Understand clearly that the body is not "mine," it belongs to the five elements, and that it is someone else's property. When you understand this, whatever kind of properties the body may possess, how does it affect you? So, let us leave the Physical Body, and let us proceed ahead. However, to leave the body does not mean that it should be pushed into a well, or be hung with a noose around the neck. We leave it by understanding it, and by gaining the factual knowledge about it. When the body is known for what it really is, the obsessive interest in it subsides, we can step beyond it, and it is automatically renounced. If the body is purposefully destroyed physically, then one definitely gets reborn again and again. Complete renunciation of the body is achieved only through discrimination of the Real from the unreal. By using discrimination while one has the human body, one naturally arrives at a state of renunciation, and instead the body becoming a reason for rebirth, it has the capacity to liberate one from the cycle of birth and death altogether.

There are five types of dissolution. Two are at the level of the body, two are at the level of the universe, and one is through discrimination.

They are:

1) Daily dissolution, or the Dissolution of Deep Sleep
2) Dissolution through Death
3) Dissolution of the Creator and Creation (Brahma Pralaya)
4) Dissolution at the time of many Ages or Kalpas (Kalpa Pralaya)
5) Dissolution by Thought, or Discrimination

Out of these five types of dissolution, everyone is familiar with the two types of dissolution associated with the body, or daily dissolution, which are Deep Sleep and the dissolution of Death. In Deep Sleep, the whole world, including our body is dissolved. However, upon awakening, the body and the world are present just as they were before going to sleep, and all actions start again, just as they did before. The dissolution through Death is the same as the dissolution through Deep Sleep, however, after Death, in the absence of Self-Knowledge, the being has to take a new body in accordance with one's actions (karma) and mental disposition. In the new body, the actions such as eating, sleeping, mating, and fear happen according to the impressions remaining from previous lives.

Above the bodily level at the universal level there are two other cosmic types of dissolution. The first is the dissolution at the end of the life of the Creator and his Creation (Brahma Pralaya). The second is the dissolution that takes place at the end of an age or "Kalpa" after many such Creators and their Creations have come and gone (Kalpa Pralaya). With these two types of dissolution, a new "Creator," or a new "Kalpa" starts, and "Creation," which was latent for some time, rises with renewed vigor and activity, and starts all over again. In this way, the wheel continues to revolve, rising and setting at fixed periods. One can see from the descriptions given so far of these four types of dissolutions, that bodies cannot be dissolved finally in all of them. However, the result of the dissolution by discrimination, or thought, is very powerful and unique. In this type of dissolution, the body not only is dissolved while living but also after death, and when it gets finally dissolved it will not rise again.

Suppose there is a toy snake lying around that is made out of rubber. It is only until such time that one understands that it is only made of rubber, that the fear of the snake will completely disappear. Otherwise, by closing ones eyes, or putting the snake away in a basket, the fear subsides. However, in that case, as soon as the eyes open, or the basket is opened again, the fear returns. Suppose someone throws the rubber snake away and some mischievous person again throws it in front of the fearful one. He will again be shaken. In order to escape the snake, the man goes into Deep Sleep, however he will see the snake again as soon as he wakes up. Suppose he gets intoxicated with drink, or is made unconscious by chloroform in order to make the snake go away. Again, as soon as the effect of the drink or anesthesia wears off, the snake is there once again. This shows that the eradication of the fear of the snake by any of the means described is only temporary and not lasting. How is it then that he can be freed from the fear of the snake? The only remedy to be rid of the fear of the snake, is to know for certain that it is only made of rubber.

Once this knowledge dawns, then even if his eyes see the snake, or if somebody wants to frighten him with it, there is no cause for fear. In the same way, when one knows correctly as to exactly what this body is, the "pride" for it and the sense of "mine" about it vanishes and it is automatically renounced. This is what is called the "dissolution by thought." One who dies with this certainty of thought is free from the cycle of births and deaths. However, it should be taken for granted that one who dies "thoughtlessly," dies only in order to be reborn. By virtue of the "dissolution by thought," the thing is seen as if it were immaterial, whether it is or is not there. With the other types of dissolution, even if the thing is hidden from sight, it is just as if it still exists. Samartha Ramdas therefore asserts that it is only "thoughtfulness" (Vichara) that makes a human being complete, and brings one to fulfillment in life. After thorough investigation, the "I" could not be found when the Physical Body was dissected with the procedure of "dissolution by thought."

The Second Body - The Subtle Body

Now we will use the same process of "dissolution by thought" in trying to trace the "I" in the Subtle Body. Let us investigate and see if this thief called "I" can be found anywhere in the Subtle Body. First, let us first find out what the Subtle Body is.

The Subtle Body is comprised of a committee of seventeen members. These are:

1. The Five Senses of Action (hands, feet, mouth, genitals, and anus),
2. The Five Senses of Knowledge (eyes, ears, nose, tongue, and skin),
3. The Five Pranas or vital breaths (vyana vayu which supplies liquid food materials throughout the body, samana vayu which is found in the navel, udana vayu which is found in the throat, apana vayu which is found in the bowels, and prana vayu which is what we breath in and out),
4. The Mind (Manas), and
5. The Intellect (Buddhi)

Whatever orders that this committee of the Subtle Body puts forth are carried out by the Gross Body. The Subtle Body's "field of authority" is very vast, so in conducting a thorough investigation, it may be possible to find that elusive "I" here because he has a strong passion for asserting authority. When we begin our investigation of the Subtle Body, we find that the "I" puts his stamp of "mine" here also. Whatever is found here is labeled as "my senses," "my pranas," "my mind," "my intellect." However, upon closer examination, no such sound as "I am the intellect" is ever heard. That "I" parades around as the "owner" here in the Subtle Body also, but is nowhere to be found. Thus, according to the same reasoning used previously that "There can be nothing which I can call 'mine' where 'I' am not present," the Subtle Body, nor any of its collective members (the senses, the Pranas, the mind, or the intellect) can be "me."

There is an objection that can be raised to this logic of "Where I am not, there can be nothing which I can call my own." For example, King George the 5th is not present in Sholapur. Does it then follow that Sholapur is not under his ownership? The answer to this objection is thus: At least there is an individual who is called George the 5th, and even if he is living elsewhere, he can have ownership in Sholapur even though he is presently not there. However, this "I" is a "non-entity," and like "Mr. Gomaji Ganesh" from the example earlier, the proliferation of its arrogance and ignorance has remained unexamined, and this "I" is claiming authority here in the Subtle Body as well. When the "I" cannot be traced, how can there be anything there that can be claimed as "mine" to be sustained by the Subtle Body?

The Subtle Body is like a subtle silk bundle. Even though it is more difficult to untie the subtle silk knot with thought than it was with the Gross Body, it is still necessary for the aspirant to put forth the effort to untie it. Once the bundle is untied and left open for thorough examination, the Subtle Body is automatically renounced. It is important to recognize that *the seed of birth and death is the Subtle Body itself*, which is of the nature of desire. If that seed is roasted just once in the "Fire of Knowledge," it may appear unchanged, but even if it were ever to be sown, there is no hope of it sprouting.

A doubt may arise here that if both the gross and subtle bodies are renounced, and the attitude of pride such as "I" and "mine" also disappears, is it not possible that the actions of the body may either come to a halt, or might not be executed efficiently? The doubt may be removed thus: Suppose someone keeps a thing in a locker because he is under the impression that it is made of gold. However, at some point, he finds out that instead of gold, it is really made of brass. With that recognition, he can choose to either leave it in the locker or remove it and keep it outside. His attachment to it will either vanish or become greatly diminished, and this is a fact. In the same way, if the pride of possession of the body as "mine" is ignored, nothing of value will be lost.

Saint Tukaram said, "Let the body live or die, I have complete faith in my Self Nature." If an aspirant reaches this level of conviction, the attitude arises, "When one experiences the 'Bliss of Brahman' (Brahmananda) who cares for the body?" When this attitude arises, it is truly praiseworthy. A dog once bit off a piece of flesh from Saint Kabir's calf muscle. Saint Kabir simply said, "Either the dog knows, or the flesh knows. Anything is possible." What could have been the feeling of the people around upon hearing this from Saint Kabir, who was a great devotee? The aspirant can easily see the degree of renunciation that Saint Kabir had reached. He fully understood that it was the flesh that was affected and not his True Nature.

Although this understanding that the Self remains unaffected was experienced by Saint Kabir, and also by Saint Tukaram when he lost his whole household, the aspirant might not get the same sense of unshaken ecstasy within oneself in the beginning when one initially undertakes the search for the "I." If by God's Grace, such Bliss does overwhelm you, you might say, "What are all these worldly possessions worth after all?," and you will never feel the need to ask such pointless questions as "Will my house be run properly?" At that point, you will have developed such an indifferent attitude that you will say, "Let whatever is to happen, happen, and let whatever has to go, go."

However, if the aspirant understands intellectually, which is easier than experiencing the Self, he raises the question "After the Knowledge of the Self is attained, and the possessive pride of the body and the mind is left behind, can one's worldly duties still be performed?" To console him, the Sadguru answers "Dear one, of course, even after realizing the utter uselessness of the body and mind one can establish a household and have children without bringing in the pride of the body and the mind. In fact, these things can be looked after very well. All of the relevant duties one did earlier can still be diligently performed."

How is this possible, you may ask? Understand by this example: Look at the behavior of the nurse of a motherless infant. She nurses the child, carries it around, consoles it if he cries, and nurses it back to health if he gets sick, just as she would if she were the child's actual mother. If she likes the child, she even kisses it lovingly. While doing all of this work, she does not even have the feeling that the child is her own! In spite of all that she does for the child, if the father of the child dismisses her, she at once picks up her things and gets out of the house. At the time of quitting her position, she is neither happy if the child was to put on weight, nor sad if the child were to die. The reason for this attitude is that she does not have a sense of "mine" regarding the child. However, it cannot be said that she has not performed her duty properly due to the absence of this sense of "mine."

Let us look at another example. Take the case of a trustee who manages a minor's estate worth many millions of rupees. His lack of the sense of "mine" does not hinder him in his duty, and he has been managing the estate of the minor very efficiently. If the duty is not discharged properly, the trustee is liable, and will surely suffer the consequences. The trustee does not have the feeling that the estate is "mine" and accordingly, is not affected if the estate increases in value, or if even if it is decided in a legal suit that the estate does not really even belong to the minor. His duty is to look after the estate carefully as long as it is under his management. In short, in order for one's duties to be performed properly, it is not necessary that one must have the sense of "I" or "mine" while performing them. In exactly the same way, the gross and the subtle bodies form a bundle that is rooted in the five elements, and is given as a "keepsake" which is entrusted to the human being.

As a trustee, you must look after the bundle in the best possible way. If you neglect this responsibility, you will surely suffer consequences in the form of the loss of health of both body and mind. If the trustee manages the minor's estate efficiently, and the nurse looks after the child very well, they are awarded their salaries in return. Likewise, if you look after your body and mind well, and keep them in a healthy condition, you also get a return, in the form of joy. A healthy body is definitely useful in the search for the Ultimate Truth.

All of this carrying out of one's responsibilities has to be achieved without the sense of "mine." With this attitude, even if the body becomes fat or thin, or lives or dies, there is no elation or lament. If a trustee of a minor's estate is led astray by a sense of "mine" and claims ownership and embezzles from that estate, he will be jailed. In the case of spiritual practice, the identification with the body means forgetting the Self, or killing the Self. The hope of liberation recedes for the one who is bound by the idea of being a body, even though in truth, he is only nothing but the Self.

From the above discussion, it can be understood that the usual obligations and actions of the body and mind should be fulfilled in a proper manner, and that it is not necessary to establish a sense of "ownership," or a concept of "mine" in relation to them. The obligations of the trustee and the nurse while carrying out their responsibilities do not require them to have any sense of possession, and their duties are performed quite normally. In the same manner, the duties of a human being can be performed without entertaining the sense of possession, or any concept of "mine" in relation to the Physical or Subtle Bodies

The Third Body - The Causal Body

Suppose we lose the concept of possession for the Gross Body, as well as the Subtle Body, and admit to the fact that the bundle belongs to a stranger. Still, we must find the answer to the question "Who am I?" or, "Where am I?" Let us now go over the definition of the Causal Body. What is the Causal Body? As soon as we step in here, there is pitch darkness everywhere. Is it possible that this dark Ignorance is the place of residence for this "I"? It surely seems this is his main headquarters. Ignorance seems to be the main property or quality that belongs to him. There is certainly some hope of finding the elusive "I" here. Let us see.

Here we move about as if blindfolded searching for it, and the "I" is not to be found anywhere in Causal Body. Here the "I" seems to have even given up his sense of "mine." There seems nothing that can be called "mine" in this place. Everything seems to be absolutely quiet. That "I" who loudly proclaims "I, I" so arrogantly in the gross and subtle bodies, seems to be totally silent here. The "I" seems to be playing hide and seek so that he does not get caught by the one who searches for it. In the Causal Body, the "I" seems to have dug itself into a trench of darkness so that the one making the search might fall in, being forced to end his search.

Dear aspirants, do not be concerned. The Sadguru is standing behind you as well as in front of you, and He will take you safely across this trench of darkness. Many scholars and learned persons have turned their backs at this point and abandoned their search failing to have faith in the guidance of the Sadguru. For you however, there is no reason to abandon your search like them. You have a guide who is a very capable Master, a Samartha Sadguru. (The word Samartha means "The Powerful One who knows His Own Significance," in the highest sense.)

After stabilizing in this darkness of the Causal Body, and firmly planting one's feet therein for some period of time, a voice is softly heard that says, "I am the witness of this Ignorance." With this, there arises some courage offering the hope of catching the thief called "I." With the recognition of this voice who says it is the witness of the Ignorance, there also comes the thought "This thief is here somewhere. He may be near, or a little further ahead, but he is witnessing the Ignorance from somewhere nearby." Here the searching takes the form of watching persistently. How this is done will be discussed in the next chapter. The witnessing that is going on is happening from beyond the emptiness of the Causal Body, from the position in the Great-Causal Body (Mahakarana Body), or Turya State. When this is understood, the "I" is quickly overjoyed in finding himself. Who can describe that Joy? In that Joy, the "I" cries out "I am Brahman, I am Self-Knowledge."

The Fourth Body - The Great-Causal Body (Turya)

The one who says "I" is really the all-witnessing Brahman. It is He, who is of the nature of Knowledge, the sense of "I Am." When this certainty is established, there arises wave after wave of Bliss. Afterwards, when this Bliss ebbs away, look at the miracle that happens. After enquiry and deep thought (Vichara), one arrives at the recognition that, "I am not even of the nature of 'Knowledge,' for just as I am covered with 'Ignorance,' in the same way, I am covered with 'Knowledge.' I was not originally having any Ignorance or Knowledge. Ignorance and Knowledge were born out of 'me,' and were mistakenly taken to be 'me.' With the aid of such deep thought, it can be seen that the arising of both Ignorance and Knowledge within 'me,' points to 'me' as their creator. Therefore Knowledge is my child, and I am its father, and as its father, I am prior to, and different from, that Knowledge."

Brahman

When this sequence of deep discriminative thought dawns within, the sense that "I am Brahman," (Aham Brahmasmi) that is the Self-Knowledge in the Great-Causal Body, or Turya State, also starts ebbing away, only to finally be fully eradicated. Then "I" am absolutely naked, without any covering whatsoever. Arriving here in this nakedness, it cannot be described as to who or what this "I," is. If you want a description of the "I" who is found here, you may utter any word found in any dictionary, but that is not "I." This "I" here, can only be expressed as "Not this, not this." It is the one who throws light on anything called "this." You may utter words and sentences to try to describe it, but those are not it. Whatever meanings come forth, you take those to be the description of "I," but those are not it. If you do not understand what is being told now, you must leave off the words and concepts, and merge in Deep Silence, and see who "I" am.

Chapter 3: Investigation of the Four Bodies in Detail

A Methodical Approach to Explanation

So far, during the search for the "I," we turned the four bodies inside out and could not find a trace of it. It is true that the "I" disappeared without words beyond the four bodies, where even the ideas of "I" and "you" do not exist. However, it will not do to just keep quiet, and mistake this for Deep Silence. In the exposition thus far, the Gross, the Subtle, the Causal, and the Great-Causal bodies have been superficially described. It is necessary to examine in detail all aspects of the four bodies. Unless these are fully understood correctly and this understanding is made a part of one's nature, an aspirant will not be able to arrive at this Deep Silence, which is Reality. We will therefore examine in detail what the aspects of the four bodies are.

It is necessary to understand that these four bodies are the four steps that one must ascend in order to proceed on to the fifth rung of Deep Silence which is "Nihshabda," where the "word" becomes silent. Going step by step, one can surely reach the end of the journey. However, if some steps are missed, and one puts one's foot on the next step prematurely, there is a likelihood of losing one's balance, and falling back. Therefore it is only when one body is fully understood that the aspirant should continue on to the next body. Without using this methodical approach, if one starts stepping up the steps too hastily, there will be confusion. In this confusion, true understanding will not be gained, and the aspirant will likely misunderstand the subtle differences between Deep Sleep and Samadhi, as well as those of Ignorance as Knowledge.

By way of comparison, consider the difference between a toy top that is still when it is not moving and when it appears to be still due to intense speed, or the difference between total darkness and the blackout that is caused by intense light. Although these things appear similar from a casual glance or superficial perspective, there is a vast difference between the two states, and their usefulness or capacity is also different. If one works methodically step by step to gain understanding, there will be no confusion as to the subtle differences that are being indicated. Here it is prudent to bring to the attention of the reader the method of exposition of a subject that is provided in the ancient scriptures. This will convince the aspirant that there is no basis for any doubts to arise regarding any apparent contradictions in the method adopted for the exposition of some particular point in the scriptures. Therefore, we must first describe the method of expounding the teaching that has been adopted by the ancient scriptures (This is often referred to as the "primary premise" presented in the Vedas).

When a subject is to be explained to an aspirant, there is first a description of the subject matter, showing its great importance. It is then explained that a great reward will follow if the subject matter is correctly understood. Once the aspirant understands the subject completely, before moving on and explaining the next subject, the instructor using the scriptural method is to first impress upon the aspirant the uselessness of the subject that has already been understood. Only after that can the importance of the subject to be taught next be impressed upon him. The reason for this method is that there is no inclination for one to strive to understand a subject unless its importance is first brought out, with a promise of some reward, as a motivation. Next, the uselessness of the subject matter just learned is brought home to the aspirant so that the subject is automatically renounced, and the aspirant becomes eager to understand what is to be presented as the next topic.

The Mother Shruti (the Vedas) takes into consideration the psychological background of an aspirant, and then inspires him to work for food, first telling him that the food is Brahman. She then gives him time to fondle the Gross Body, telling him that the Gross Body is Brahman. Then it is explained that all experiences of joy that come to the Gross Body are actually enjoyed by the Subtle Body. The Gross Body is shown to be merely a corpse, and it is told how the corpse could in no way enjoy anything if it were not for the Subtle Body. Thus, the uselessness of the Gross Body is demonstrated.

Next, the mind, intellect, senses, and the sheath that makes up the Pranas (vital breaths) are described, and this Subtle Body is said to be Brahman. It is shown to be bigger or more expansive than the Gross Body. In this way, the Vedas give importance to the Subtle Body. After that, comes the description of the Causal Body, which is still, and even more expansive than the Subtle Body. It swallows the Subtle Body. The Causal Body is then proclaimed to be Brahman and the advice is given to the aspirant that "You yourself have become the expansive Causal Body." However, since the Causal Body is considered to be Ignorance and in total darkness, the final claim of it being the Self cannot really be made here. Accordingly, the aspirant is therefore compelled to investigate further, into the Great-Causal Body. This Great-Causal Body is still more expansive, and it is from here that the voice saying "I am the witness" emanates. Upon arriving here, the Great-Causal Body, or Turya State, is investigated and examined thoroughly.

In this way, the Mother Vedas dismiss each body after having asserted that it was Brahman. When she is finally confronted with the problem of explaining the changeless, attributeless Brahman (Nirguna Brahman) she claims an inability to describe it, and only keeps repeating the sentence, "Not this, Not this. That which is not 'Ignorance,' and that which is not 'Knowledge' is Brahman, and that which you call 'Brahman,' is not Brahman." In such a negative way, Mother Shruti describes Brahman as "That" which is beyond all of the four bodies.

The principle of what has just been described is as follows: When it said that one body is bigger than the previous body it does not mean that it is higher in relation to it, etc. In a comparison of needles for example, the needle used for stitching jute bags is bigger that one used for cotton, but it is not bigger than an iron rod that is used for digging. This indicates that qualities like "bigger" and "smaller" are not inherent in a thing, but are imposed upon it by relating it to or comparing it with some other thing. The same rule applies here. After listing in sequence first food as Brahman, then Gross Body as Brahman, then Subtle Body as Brahman, then the Causal, and finally the Great-Causal Body as Brahman, and in each case, the latter being greater than the former, the intention is to give the instruction and demonstrate the principle that out of all these, ultimately none can be said to be Brahman. Although it is shown that in each case that the latter state is relatively higher or more expansive than the previous one, it is still not Brahman, and moreover, this Parabrahman is absolutely unique and beyond all of these four bodies.

While utilizing the above-mentioned method of explaining a point, it is necessary to understand clearly just what it is that is being described as Brahman. Why is it that it should be described in this way? How far can one go to describe it as being with some particular qualities? Moreover, why is it that what was once called Brahman, is then negated as not being Brahman in the same breath? *It is very important to understand this correctly.* For example, in giving instruction on how to cook rice to a person who is not a proper cook, the person is told to first light a fire under the utensil in which the rice is being cooked. After some time, another instruction is given to the same person to put the fire out now. It is natural that the person may wonder about the contradictory instructions. His teacher explains to him, "Dear one, it is necessary to keep a fire under the utensil until the rice is cooked, but later, the fire has to be put out, otherwise we would get coals instead of rice."

This is the reason why any method to be practiced is necessary only until its goal is achieved. Otherwise, it will only bring on exhaustion and nothing further beneficial will be achieved. Thus, when the Subtle Body being called as Brahman is thoroughly examined and understood, the merit of calling the Subtle Body as Brahman loses its value, and it becomes necessary to move on, and continue the search for "I" by examining the next thing. This demonstrates that sometimes when we offer a price for something, or place some value on it in order to achieve some particular results, that value that we have placed on it may not necessarily be the real value of that thing. For example, some occasion may arise in one's life where you might have to address even a donkey as uncle. In this example, the honor that is given to the donkey is due to some consequence you must endure for some action done.

In the same way, some great calamity that someone may be facing is because he has forgotten his real nature. It is therefore necessary to become liberated from the calamity or obstruction, which is like being caught in the jaws of a crocodile. If you free yourself from the crocodile by flattery saying that her back is very smooth, does it really mean that her back is as soft as a feather mattress? This question should be asked of the man who gets released from the crocodile's jaws. To rid oneself of the crocodile like grip of the four bodies, they are called Brahman for some short period of time. Taking into account that this is the method of explanation that will be used, we will now turn our attention to the actual explanation and description of the four bodies.

The Investigation Commences

The nature of the Gross Body is quite well known. It is a mass of flesh and blood that can be touched with the hand, and all are quite familiar with it. Not only that, but everyone uses it fully. The Gross Body is "I" and therefore all the passions and desires that happen to the body are "mine." Accordingly, the dark or fair complexion of the body, and the stages of childhood, youth, and old age, belong to "me." The relationship of the body to caste, religion, house, land, and wealth, are all "mine." This is a lesson that every human being has learned through many births, and he has learned it very well. In fact, it is so well learned that even while dreaming, someone will tell you that he is "so-and-so." It is therefore not necessary to teach anyone this lesson that has been repeatedly learned over and over, and has been so firmly implanted in one's psyche. The feet of all human beings are resting steadily on the step of this Gross Body. The state of this Gross Body is that of "wakefulness" and in this body, there is partial forgetfulness and partial remembrance. The quality of worldly action, or "Rajoguna," is predominant in the Gross Body. This basic explanation is enough for one to understand the Gross Body. We will now turn to the next step, that of the Subtle Body.

As has been previously stated, the Subtle Body is a committee. It is a collection of the senses, the Pranas, the mind, the intellect, seated on the "Inner-mind" (Antahkarana), which collectively create a type of mental world or "dream world" that is seen when the visible world becomes invisible when closing the eyes. After some thought and investigation, it can be noticed that the Subtle Body is really a very peculiar thing. Upon examination, it can be seen that all of the movements of the Gross Body are according to the dictates of this Subtle Body. The assertion of a concept, such as "something is like this," is called "Sankalpa," and a doubt, or the notion that "something is not like this" is called "Vikalpa." This Subtle Body is such that it is always presenting this perverse type of knowledge of contradictory thoughts, and its state is that of "dreaming." Continuous memory is the indicative quality of the Subtle Body, and the quality of "awareness" or "Sattvaguna" is the quality that is predominant here.

After being introduced to the Subtle Body in this way the aspirant becomes that body. When one foot is planted firmly on the next step, the other foot is lifted from the previous step, and placed beside the first foot. In this way, one leaves the first step completely. When one crosses the boundaries of a village and puts his foot within the limits of the next village, the first village is left behind, and one becomes a traveler to the next village. Similarly, in order to understand properly the step of the Subtle Body described above, when the aspirant plants his foot firmly on this step he has to lift his foot from the Gross Body in order to bring this understanding into practice. When the Gross Body is left behind, the aspirant then has to sever all connections with it.

However, this work is not so easily done, as it seems that for crossing over these steps, every human being has only two legs. One leg is the leg of learning, and the other is the leg of putting into practice what one has learned. Taking both feet away from the step of the Gross Body and planting them on the step of the Subtle Body means that one has to transcend the Physical Body. When one leaves behind the sense of pride and possession of the Gross Body and takes up the pride of possession in the Subtle Body, he has to say, "I am only the Subtle Body." Only when this is experienced does it mean that the Gross Body has been renounced and the Subtle Body is now accepted as "I." When the aspirant comes to this second step, then the lower step is left behind and one now accepts that the Gross Body is not "I." The "I" has no relationship with the Gross Body. The changes that happen to the Gross Body and its qualities, such as having a dark or fair complexion are no longer considered as "mine." No qualities of the Gross Body belong to me, as I am only the Subtle Body. This means that the qualities of the Subtle Body such as the senses, the

Pranas, the mind, the intellect, the sense of "I am," etc. are not endowed with gross physical qualities such as fat or thin, dark or fair, young or old, etc. It is clear that "I" am only the mind and the intellect, etc., with subtle qualities. If the aspirant studies this diligently, then both feet become firmly planted on the second step and he loses the sense of pride in, and identification with, the Gross Body. He becomes indifferent to all qualities and conditions of the Gross Body.

The third step is above and beyond the Subtle Body, and is the Causal Body, or "Ignorance." The Causal Body is a state of pure "Forgetfulness" where the quality of Ignorance or "Tamoguna" is predominant. Here in the Causal Body, there is no thought as to the well being of, or any relationship with, either the Gross or the Subtle Bodies. The Causal Body means that there is no knowledge of anything. It is like the state of Deep Sleep, but it is not Deep Sleep. The Causal Body is difficult to understand, *however it cannot be overstated that it is very important to understand this state.* Those who proclaim to understand the principle of zero (nothingness; the void) came to this state and turned back saying that there was nothing ahead.

The Causal Body is the state of the "unknowable" or "the void" which is presented in the point of view of Western Philosophers. This state which is devoid of all thoughts, imagination, and doubts, is often mistakenly taken by aspirants to be Samadhi, and thought to be the same as Brahman without concepts or qualities (Nirvikalpa Brahman). When this void or state of emptiness is reached, one is likely to get a false satisfaction and say, "Today I saw Brahman." The interval or pause between where one modification of the mind disappears, and another one does not arise (such as the space between two thoughts, or the intervening pause between when sleep sets in and the waking state disappears) is a state of pure forgetfulness. This is what is described as the "Covering of Bliss" (Anandamaya Kosha) in the scriptures. In the Causal Body all chaos, struggle, and the infinite number of waves of thought have ceased. Therefore, there is a sense of peace in this third body that is not found in the other two bodies. It is true that the aspirant experiences a certain joy, but this is not Ultimate Peace, or even true Bliss. One must understand this point very well. This Causal Body is the natural state of all the gods, demons, and every human being. The state of the Causal Body is the state of "Forgetfulness."

The chief sign or indication of the Causal Body is to forget everything. For example, unless one forgets everything he cannot get Deep Sleep. To say "I was asleep, but I remembered something," is to really say, "I never slept." To really have Deep Sleep means not to remember a single thing. Similarly, to forget everything while in an awakened state, is to enter the Causal Body. To be in a state where you do not know anything, is to also come to this state. As previously mentioned, this is the natural state of a human being. Even the most learned scholars do not understand the nature of a human being, let alone the nature of Shiva. In order for one to fully understand this state of human forgetfulness, the method of studying the pause is prescribed. If anything is very difficult, it is to be completely stabilized in the state of forgetfulness, and to know it thoroughly. *To achieve this is very important in one's spiritual progress, and takes great effort on the part of the aspirant.* The Saints have put particular emphasis on this point.

The pause between two states is nothing but Pure Consciousness. The state of the "mouni" (a silent one) is such that he does not allow a single word to rise, or even if it did rise, he does not allow its meaning to rise, but simply lets it slip by. When the word rises, and is allowed to impress its meaning on the "inner-mind," the world is born. Ignoring the word, and not allowing it to carry any meaning for the mind, is the eradication of the world. When the word does not energize the mind, what remains is the "Pure Energy of Consciousness." To experience this state continuously is called "The State of Silence."

The aspirant who is about to put his foot on the third step after climbing the first and second, is told that this step is the state of Pure Consciousness. He is under the impression that this state is the Pure Void, and taking this void to be Brahman, he is unable to witness the void. However, when the aspirant proceeds to the fourth step, he begins to look back at the third step. Being unable to see anything in the void of the Causal Body he wonders why the Guru has instructed him to put his foot on this step of nothingness which doesn't exist at all. The reason is, that once Pure Consciousness is known, there can be no trace of anything that is called "Ignorance," so one does not come to understand what the state of "Forgetfulness" is, and there does not arise any modification in the aspirant's mind except that of Pure Consciousness.

Knowledge, or Consciousness presents itself to the aspirant in two ways:

> 1. When there is an object in Consciousness it becomes "Objective Knowledge" and one will experience it as knowledge of objects.
>
> 2. When there is no object, it is experienced as objectless Knowledge, or "Pure Consciousness."

When there is an object, that is called "Objective Knowledge." When there is no object, that is simply "Knowledge," which is Pure Awareness, or Consciousness. With the exception of these two (Objective Knowledge and Pure Knowledge), no other modifications are present in the aspirant's mind. In Pure Consciousness, the word "Ignorance" is meaningless from the aspirant's point of view. It is not possible for Forgetfulness to exist in his case. Whatever is experienced will either be Objective Knowledge, or Pure Consciousness that is without any objects.

Presenting the state of the Causal Body to the aspirant that it is just Ignorance, a void, a state of Forgetfulness, or something where there is nothing to bring home to him, is to lead him to the above fact of Pure Consciousness. By analogy, a teacher will draw on the blackboard a point of great length and breadth in order to teach the student about a point that has neither length nor breadth. Similarly, this is how the point is being illustrated here. If it is not done in this manner, the next step cannot be explained. The aspirant should therefore have full faith in the Sadguru without further argument and take it for granted that there is a state of Forgetfulness. He should thus commence practicing what is being told, and begin the process of forgetting each and every thing. It must be understood that the casual body is the cause of the two previous bodies. Hence the label "Causal Body."

Here the example is given of the side curtain on a theater stage, which is called the wing, from which the actors emerge and where they again disappear back into. The Causal Body, which is the natural state of a human being, is like this wing on the stage, and exists in the state of the form of "Forgetfulness." From behind this curtain, all memories appear and then disappear. When we say that we have forgotten a thing before remembering it, this means that the thing was abiding there in that state of Forgetfulness, and it is proved that it has emerged from that state alone. In opposition to this, when we say that we forgot a certain thing, this means that the thing that was in memory has disappeared behind this curtain of Forgetfulness. A memory before it is forgotten, and something forgotten after it is remembered, are companions in this arena of Forgetfulness. The rising and setting of all ideas are in the womb of this one "Forgetfulness," which is the common ground for all human beings. It is by reason of this Forgetfulness that each human being feels he is ignorant, and strives to obtain knowledge. During this struggle, the majority unfortunately only gain worldly knowledge, thus missing the "Knowledge of their True Nature."

When introducing the Causal Body in the manner described above, the Sadguru tells the disciple, "Dear one, you are not the Gross Physical Body, and you are not the Subtle Body, so you should identity yourself with the Causal Body." For an aspirant to be in the state of "Forgetfulness," it means that he should have the feeling that "I am definitely not the Gross Body, and I am not the Subtle Body. Therefore, all of the dreams and doubts that arise in the Subtle Body, do not reside in me. I am complete 'Forgetfulness,' empty of all concepts and imaginings. The birth and death of the body, the miseries and temptations, the pain and pleasure, as well as the hunger and thirst that arise in the Pranas, cannot touch me. Honor and dishonor are only notions in the mind, and qualities such as fair or dark complexion belong to the Physical Body, but I am none of these. Nothing can attach itself to me. I am Forgetfulness."

Committing oneself to this lesson again and again and becoming firmly established in the state of Forgetfulness without any idea or attachment, it becomes our own nature. In this way, one experiences oneself as being completely empty of all of the qualities of the Gross and the Subtle Bodies. When this practice of experiencing oneself as Forgetfulness is firmly established the aspirant definitely rises to the third step. Becoming steady in this Forgetfulness, the aspirant is worthy of proceeding to the next step, to the Great-Causal Body (the Mahakarana Body), the Turya State.

However, before going to the next step, it is necessary to mention that the Causal Body although similar to Deep Sleep, is a state quite distinct from sleep. In Deep Sleep, all of the senses are in complete repose with the complete absence of any activity, and consequently any perception of sense objects. In Deep Sleep, all beings enjoy the bliss of being in their own nature, but do not really know their True Nature. Upon awakening from Deep Sleep, everyone will say these two sentences: "I slept happily," and "I did not know anything." Like this, everyone conveys the contentment and bliss of their own nature, as well as their ignorance regarding it. In this manner, although one unknowingly conveys their awareness of Ignorance, it also proves the existence of a deeper Awareness. However, this does not mean that one was aware of their true Self, even though they were experiencing it during Deep Sleep. During Deep Sleep, one does not experience the Awareness that is present there. For example, suppose that there is a person who is unknowingly an heir to a treasure of buried gold coins. Everyday he goes to sleep on the ground and does his normal begging in the morning for his livelihood. For him, the treasure is as good as not being there at all. Similarly, each human being goes into and comes out of their true nature, diving deep and experiencing bliss. However the deep ignorance about one's real nature is there as part of that experience. It is for this reason that Deep Sleep cannot be the means of gaining "Self-Knowledge," the Knowledge of one's "True Nature." In Deep Sleep, the aspirant has no ability to study that state. However, this is not the case with regard to the state of "Forgetfulness."

To study Forgetfulness is to enjoy the state of Deep Sleep while being fully awake. The manner in which to enjoy this wakeful Deep Sleep is taught by the Sadguru. How does a fish sleep while living in water? One can only understand this if you get a birth in that species. How can the sleep of a fish not be disturbed by the water entering into his eyes? This secret is known only when one is born as a fish. In the same way, how can one experience and understand this Deep Sleep state while one is fully awake? One can only understand this by becoming a true Son of the Sadguru, a "Guruputra."

The Causal Body, which is of the nature of Forgetfulness is nothing but a very deep sleep. However, that which is described above, is the silence within that is experienced "knowingly," or consciously, during the Waking State. It is not the Deep Sleep state that comes "unknowingly," without conscious awareness. Nothing is known in the state of Deep Sleep which comes "unknowingly." However, the nature of the Self can be known by means of employing the method of knowing "Forgetfulness" which is experienced while awake. This is the difference between "Deep Sleep," and Samadhi.

Although it is known that "Forgetfulness" is a state where nothing is known, the fact is, that after everything is forgotten "Knowledge" remains. This "Knowledge" can only be understood through the study of Forgetfulness.

This state of Forgetfulness exists, and must be understood. Deep Sleep and Forgetfulness are both the result of "Tamoguna." By way of analogy, an analysis of coal and diamond shows that both are made of carbon. This means that the coal and the diamond are but two aspects of carbon. Although this is the case, there is a vast difference in their respective values. When the ingredient of carbon is the same in both, how is it that the diamond shines and the coal is black and lusterless? The reason is that the proportion of the same component is different in the two. Likewise Deep Sleep, and Forgetfulness share different proportions of Ignorance, which explains why in Deep Sleep the immense density of Ignorance is felt, while in Forgetfulness the flimsiness of Ignorance is realized.

As the depth of Deep Sleep decreases, the onset of wakefulness arises. The man who wakes up from Deep Sleep is at first slightly under the fuzzy influence of sleep, and then awakens slowly. This state is the result of the depth of sleep becoming thinner, or more flimsy, as the state of full wakefulness emerges and sleep ends. Deep Sleep is like a pitch black curtain which covers the lamp of the Self, while the Causal Body or the state of Forgetfulness that is being examined is like a thin transparent velvet curtain. This means that the enjoyment of bliss is the same in both Deep Sleep and the Causal Body (Forgetfulness). However, from the point of view of achieving the knowledge of one's True Nature, Deep Sleep is useless. It is like attempting to procreate by having sexual intercourse with a barren woman. The study of this "Sheath of Bliss," (Anandamaya Kosha) in the form of the state of Forgetfulness provides one with joy and is a necessary step in reaching the goal of knowing one's "True Nature."

Having said all of this, we will now observe the Great-Causal Body, or the Turya State, which is endowed with the "Knowledge" that comes after the study of Forgetfulness. Here, let us digress a little. Those aspirants who have taken the traditional Mantra, according to the tradition of Shri Sadguru Bhausaheb Maharaj may have doubts at this point. The study of the Causal Body means that one should learn to forget everything. Does this also mean that repeating the Mantra given by the Guru, and the color or forms that stand before one's half-closed eyes should also be forgotten? The answer is Yes! You have to do this. Before doing this, while repeating the Mantra, the colors and whatever forms are present, so the aspirant must check for oneself that the mental noises and chatter cease and die out completely.

When concentrating on the tip of the nose with half-closed eyes in a relaxed manner, with the exception of the repetition of the Mantra and the color form, there should not arise any other word or form. This having been done, even that has to be forgotten. The broom in one's hand that is used to sweep out the rubbish in the house should not be kept in the hand after the rubbish has been cleaned out from every corner of the house. The broom also has to be thrown out in the end. The Sadguru imparts the Mantra to the aspirant as a discipline. He gives a tool in the form of the Mantra which sweeps clean all rubbish in the form of doubts, fears, imaginings, and concepts that have been accumulated over the infinite number of births. This tool of the Mantra helps the aspirant learn how to concentrate, or focus his attention, and enables the mind to become subtle. How the tool should be utilized, and when it should be left alone, has now been been clearly explained.

Now, we will see what the fourth body, the Great-Causal Body is. (The Great-Causal Body is also known in the teachings of Vedanta as the Turya State, or SatChitAnanda. It is called Great-Causal because it is above, or beyond the limits of the Causal Body.) It is the father of the other three bodies. In Hindu mythology, King Janaka (Janaka means Creator, or Producer) was one without a body (Videhi). He had a daughter named Janaki (Janaki means Awareness). This mythological story tells us that King Janaka is the same as the fourth body, the Great-Causal Body. This indicates a state of Consciousness that is without a body in spite of the fact that the body still exists. That is the state of "Knowledge" in the fourth body. This is King Janaka. Out of him, the daughter Janaki (Awareness) is created. Compared with the previous three bodies, the fourth body is a state that is without a body, and without any conditions, in the form of "Knowledge." However, this does not mean that there is an absence of Knowledge found in the previous three bodies.

Knowledge is the same whether it is in an agitated condition or in equanimity. It is clean and pure in the state of equanimity as well as in the disturbed condition, even when immersed in the flood of objective knowledge. In all states, Knowledge is One and the same. However, the knowledge in the first three bodies is adulterated knowledge, or conditional objective knowledge. The Knowledge in the state of the Great-Causal Body is balanced with an intermingling of the three gunas (Rajas, Tamas, and Sattva), and can be experienced as "Pure Knowledge."

Whether Knowledge is in a balanced or an unbalanced state, Knowledge is always Knowledge. However, it is different with respect to it's conditioning. Because of the identification with particular conditionings of Knowledge, a human being sees differences, and creates distinctions and separateness in the One Knowledge. For example, the sweetness that one tastes in the various sweets called laddoos, or jilebis, or basundis, is all sugar. However, because it is in these particular forms we say that the laddoo is sweet, the jilebi is sweet, or the basundi is sweet. If we taste some sugar that is not mixed with any other ingredients, we will say that sugar is sweet. If someone is given a description of what sugar is like, and is given a laddoo and told that the sweetness in the laddoo is sugar, he will never get the knowledge of the true nature of sugar. However, if he is given pure sugar unmixed with any other ingredients he will know exactly what sugar is.

This example illustrates why Knowledge cannot be experienced in its primal state in the first three bodies because it is always in some form of conditioning. In the first three bodies it will always be experienced only as objective knowledge. In the Fourth Body, that Knowledge which is "non-objective" and Pure, and which is not apparent (visible) in the other three bodies, shines in its "Pure Nature." This is the reason why aspirants have to be taken to the Great-Causal Body. When Pure Knowledge, or Consciousness, is known, then even if it is mixed with objective knowledge, or is in any other state, the aspirant will understand correctly that the entity that is called "the world," is not separate, or different from that which is called "The Knowledge of the Self" (Self-Knowledge).

Even when each state comes and goes, the witness of these states does not come or go anywhere. The one who sees the dark and fair complexion, as well as childhood, youth, and old age, of the Physical Body, is also the one who sees all concepts, imaginings, dreams, and doubts in the Subtle Body. The same witness also sees the Causal Body where there is a complete absence of concepts, imagination, and doubts. The one who witnesses all three of these bodies is forever awake.

There is a story of a woman with a peculiar characteristic who delivered a child. The child died before it knew its mother, and never saw the faces of its brother or sister that were also dead. This woman had many such children who died. The woman however remained where she was after burying all of the children. Not one child saw the face of another child, but the woman had seen all of the faces of the children, and had within her a recognition of all those children. This is exactly like the three bodies that were born of the Great-Causal Body, which is in the form of the Primal Illusion (MoolaMaya). However, none of these three bodies ever had the chance of seeing the face of each other, or the face of their mother.

Even while one state penetrates into the other, the Knowledge present in all these states is never adulterated. Just as in the example of the thread which supports all beads equally where one bead does not penetrate into the other, the Great-Causal Body is like that, as it pervades all the other states like Deep Sleep, Dream, and the Waking State. The state of Awareness, or Consciousness in the Great-Causal Body is the "Self-Luminous Flame" which becomes naked without any covering whatsoever, by making Ignorance forget itself.

Once the nature of the "Witnessing Knowledge" is known, the state of Ignorance vanishes completely. Though it is true that Ignorance vanishes, it is not true that the appearance of "the seen," or "manifestation," also vanishes. It is only the attitude, or the understanding of the aspirant that changes. By virtue of the intensity of the study, we will experience that all that is seen and appears, is in the form of "Knowledge." As soon one gains the understanding that it is only "Gold" that is perceived in a piece of jewelry, the piece of jewelry itself is not destroyed. Similarly, when it is known that everything that exists is only "The Lord of the Universe" the visible universe is not destroyed, just as when the light of a lamp destroys darkness, the objects that become known do not vanish. At first there was no light, and nothing was known beyond the fact that there were some objective forms. The nature of the objects simply became clearly known in the light. In the same way, when we were looking at and feeling the world with blind eyes in the darkness of Ignorance, the Sadguru's advice brings correct vision to our sight.

When the Flame of Knowledge is lit in the "Inner-Consciousness," it spreads light all around and the darkness of Ignorance is destroyed, yet the world appearance remains, as its True Nature is uncovered and revealed. In this way, the point of view from which one was viewing the world changes after one acquires "True Knowledge." A mirage is viewed differently from the perspective of a man and that of a deer. The object is the same, but the seeing of it is different in each case. When sand in the desert, or a road stretching out into the distance becomes hot from the sun's rays, the heat waves that rise will appear to be a body of water to someone standing far away. This appearance is called a mirage. In Marathi language, the mirage is called Mrugjala. The meaning of this is "an appearance of water at a distance that entices a deer." The reason for this name is that the deer is deceived by the mirage, and imagines it to really be water, and runs towards it to quench its thirst. Upon realizing the absence of water, the deer becomes disillusioned. It is the limited capacity of the deer's intellect that leads it to believe the appearance of water is true, and although it looks like water, a thirsty man will not run towards it to quench his thirst. The reason for this is that the mirage is not what it appears to be, and the man understands this. He is not deceived into believing that there is the presence of water there. This is the capacity of the human intellect for discerning the True from the untrue. From the point of view of the sun, there is nothing like a mirage. From where does the appearance of a mirage arise? It is similar to this that the attitude of an aspirant who is ignorant and therefore bound, and the attitude of a Siddha, or a "Liberated Man," are different. The one who is bound is driving the cart of practical duties taking it for granted that the world is true. When an aspirant gains the "Knowledge of the Self," he looks at the world with the attitude that it is just a temporary appearance or an illusion. However, the Siddha is one who has become "The Self of All," and does not see the world at all.

At this point, the first part of the exposition of the teaching, and everything regarding the Physical Gross Body up through the Great-Causal Body has been included. The next part of the teaching that is given after the explanation of the Great-Causal Body, is the teaching of the Final Reality. A person cannot be called a Siddha even if he gains Self-Knowledge by becoming identified with the Great-Causal Body (SatChitAnanda) and has realized that state.

Even though he is accomplished, he is still looked upon only as an aspirant (sadhaka). The field where the Siddhas rest is in that field of 'Supreme Knowledge" or Vijnana" (Thoughtless Reality). However, we will not discuss that yet at this point.

At this stage in the exposition, the step under our feet is the Great-Causal Body (Mahakarana Body), also known as the Turya State. First, we must discuss the Great-Causal Body in more detail. We have said that the Great-Causal Body is the state of the annihilation of Ignorance. However, it should be understood that Ignorance, the state of Forgetfulness, comes into consideration only in relation to the Gross and the Subtle Bodies. Actually, it has no real existence that has to be annihilated by acquiring "Knowledge."

It is ridiculous to say that Ignorance, or "that which is not," has to be annihilated. For example, Rama has a ring and Govinda does not have a ring. Does the absence of a ring indicate the state of existence of a certain thing called a ring? No it does not. It is in exactly in the same way that the state of 'Forgetfulness" that is non-existent and appears only in relationship to the Gross and Subtle Bodies is an imagined state. It truly does not exist. Samartha Ramdas points out in his book **Dasbodh** that this state of Ignorance in the form of Forgetfulness is the state in which that which was "not" becomes non-existent. It is natural at this point that the question might arise, "Does the state of Self-Knowledge really exist?" The one who saw the absence of dreams, imaginings, and doubts, in the state of Forgetfulness, and knew of their absence or non-existence, is "The God of Knowledge" (Jnanadeva). It is He who witnesses the dissolution of all the modifications of Knowledge and is the one who presides over the Great-Causal Body. However, it should be clearly understood that this "Witnessing Knowledge" is also a parasite (an unwanted presence) on the "Pure Nature of the Self." This "Witnessing Knowledge" is only needed to be used to annihilate the "Ignorance" of the Causal Body which means having "no knowledge." When the "Witnessing Knowledge" of the Fourth Body is left behind, the state of

Forgetfulness is forgotten, and "Knowledge" sees only at itself. Observation of one's Self cannot be called "witnessing." The seer is called a witness when he forgets the Self and sees something objective or different from the Self. When seeing only Himself, he abides in this "Supreme Knowledge," Vijnana, which is of the nature of "The Absolute."

In that "Aloneness" one likes humming to himself "Aham Brahmasmi, I am Brahman." With that sound arising from within, even this "Knowledge" is limited, or bound, and is still caught in the Great-Causal Body. This "hum" is the Primal Illusion, the original Illusion that is of the nature of the "Three Gunas" (GunaMaya). If one wants to be rid of this Illusion, even this humming sound has to stop for that rumbling Primal Illusion (MoolaMaya) to be permanently left behind. "I am Brahman" is a very subtle sense of "I Am" that is imposed on the Self, which is actually the absence of the ego or a sense of separate self. However, even this subtle type of "I Am" is like a molecule of salt in milk, and therefore has to be eradicated. To take the false as true, is a mistaken concept, but to take the True as True is the absence of any such concept. By virtue of this statement, in the absence of all concepts, the Gross Body is "I," the Subtle Body is "I," and the Causal Body is also "I." However, as long as one continues to assert oneself to be any of these three bodies, it is certainly a mistaken concept, and a type of pride.

This having been said, the Consciousness that says "I," as "I am Brahman," can be called egolessness, or having no pride, because this "I" is upholding the Truth. Where is the falsehood in it? Actually there is nothing untrue or false in this, yet, if that "True One" goes on announcing, "I am True," or "I am Brahman," there arises a doubt about this truth. If a Brahmin (someone of the priest caste) goes on telling everybody he meets "I am a Brahmin, I am a Brahmin," the listener will say, "If this man is a Brahmin why is he repeating this? He must really be of some lower caste." In the same way, the repeated assertion of the concept "I am Brahman, I am

Brahman," shows that this Consciousness, this Knowledge in the Great-Causal Body is not free from doubt about its Real Nature. From this point of view, even the memory of the concept "I am Brahman" that reminds one of the Self, has to be erased. The Consciousness (SatChitAnanda) that is of the Great-Causal Body should be stabilized to such an extent that it is of neither memory, nor forgetfulness. Only then does the aspirant become "The Nature of Pure Knowledge and Bliss."

Even when we consider our usual daily gross experiences, we are in a natural state that is without any remembrance or forgetfulness. Does anyone have an experience like "I have forgotten myself," or "I was remembering myself"? Has anyone ever tried to prove his existence by making such efforts? We do not ever forget ourselves, nor is it necessary to remember ourselves. We are always naturally in a state that is beyond the state of remembrance or forgetfulness. That is really our True Nature. Remembrance or forgetfulness is always of something "else" that is separate from ourselves. From the basis of this truth, one should make a firm mental decision that whatever is remembered or whatever is forgotten is not "I." This should be your firm conviction that whatever is remembered or forgotten is definitely not you. When there is no memory of Self, or forgetfulness of Self, there is just being one's Self, which can be recognized as "Self-Illumination." Therefore, know that the Gross Body is not you, the Subtle Body is not you, and the Causal Body is not you. You are of the nature of Self-Knowledge, the Awareness that "I am the SatChitAnanda of the Great-Causal Body." You must constantly remain the same.

Going by the theory of progressive elimination according to the instruction given above, once the conviction of one's True Nature as "Pure Knowledge, or "I Am" is realized, the four bodies have been collectively considered using the ancient method of investigation and deductive elimination. Up until now, it has been explained that you are not the three bodies. At this point, the Vedas again turn back and now announce that all of the visible appearance of the world is the sport or play (Lila) of your own Consciousness. There is a maxim, or statement, that goes like this: "A thing that is produced is like the thing from which it was produced." For example, when water is turned into ice it is still water. For the one who only sees superficially, water has a flowing tendency while ice is solid. Water has no shape and ice has shape. However, when the substance is known, they are known to be one and the same. According to this maxim it can be understood that the world, and its Lord (Brahman), are the same. This is the teaching in the Vedas.

From the gross point of view, Earth, Water, Light, Wind (Air), and Sky (Space) appear different, but the difference is only in quality. Ice becomes Water after melting, just as the Earth gets dissolved in Water, and Water dries up by the heat of Fire. Fire, or Light is contained in the Wind, and Wind gets diffused and simply disappears in the Space. Because the Self is the womb of all these five elements, they all disappear in the Self. If these principles were absolutely different from one another, they would never have dissolved into each other as one, without any remnant of difference. Consequently, the five elements, this gross world, and the subtle world, are only the Self. The Self appears as all of the different characters and species. When a painter paints a tree, a stone, cows, buffaloes, a river, the sky, gods, demons, and human beings, they are all painted with a single thing called paint. In the same way, this spectacle appearing as the world in an infinite number of forms, is nothing but Pure Knowledge. This is the bold and convincing deduction that one must conclude.

One thing has to be mentioned at this point. It must be said that the method itself is of secondary importance, whether it is the method of deductive elimination, or that of adopting some different, or contradictory method, the main purpose of a particular method is to impart the Knowledge of the Self. When an example in math is solved by several different boys, using various methods, and their answer is the same, it becomes compulsory to accept the answer as being right. The answer is what is important, and the method of arriving at the answer is of secondary importance. That is how the Vedas view the methods being used to explain to the aspirant the nature of one's True Self. There is a snag in proving the identity of water and ice, the world and God, and gold and jewelry as being the same. Even if the gold and the ornaments are the same, the ornament could not be manufactured unless the goldsmith puts his skill to work on the gold, and water could only turn into ice by virtue of intense cold. Similarly, although the world and God are the same, the rationale still presents itself that this means that some transformation must have occurred in God. He solidified as Earth, or melted and became Water, then He dried up and became Fire, etc. In this argument, first God became the five elements, and then the world was formed out of the five elements. This is a flaw in the method of deduction, and an objection can be raised in this manner. However, Samartha Ramdas has eradicated even this objection by the sentence, "Oh Man why are you asking about a thing which does not exist at all? The world has not come into existence. The Absolute Parabrahman alone exists."

To forget one's Self is the birth of Illusion, or Maya (Ma means "is not," and Ya means "which"). Maya is that "which is not," which means that she is "that which does not exist." How can one describe this non-existent woman? Is the barren woman's son fair or dark? What is his age, his height, his breadth, his caste? How can we answer these questions about that which has not come into being? To keep a child quiet from crying, he is told "the scarecrow has come." He is quieted by the creation of the tale of a scarecrow that is not really there. After the child becomes quiet, he asks his father "Daddy, what did the scarecrow look like? How long was his beard and how long was his mustache? How big were his nose, eyes, and teeth?" What answer can the father give? Until he responds the child is not going to keep quiet. At such time, the father has to stretch the nose of the scarecrow as far as Rameshwara, and his feet up to the Netherlands, and his head has to reach the sky. Thus, saying whatever he likes, he draws a frightening picture of the scarecrow saying, "he is like this, and like that, etc., so do not cry again." This kind of description alone will match the description of Maya.

The non-existent Maya exists, and she has created this world. The Vedas tried to explain to the Jivas, the human beings, how this world was created according to the capacity of their understanding. The Vedas somehow trace the source of Maya and the world. "This is just the way it happened." It can be seen that the reasoning used in the deductive elimination method at times contradicts some other theory or method. Yet, instead of accusing the Vedas that since they tell one thing to A, and another to B, that they are deceptive and telling wrong things, it must be said that the Vedas have explained the "Knowledge of the Self" to all. By using different methods according to the capacity of the aspirant's intellect, the Vedas have eradicated their Illusion, and as to who was deceptive, the aspirants were deceiving themselves as to the real nature of this world. The mother gives wheat porridge to one child and gives roti (flat bread) to another child who is suffering from indigestion. Can you call this mother partial? That mother knows which food is beneficial according to the capacity of each child's digestion. Similarly, with regard to the Vedas, different methods are used for the different types of aspirants. They differ in intellect but they are suffering from the same disease of Samsara (belief in mundane objective existence).

"Bhava Roga" means the disease that created the idea that the world has been created. To treat this disease, the Vedas and various scriptures had to give explanation in different ways according to the aspirant's capability of understanding. Even if a fever is only one symptom, a clever doctor will give different medications according to the physical condition of the patient. The doctor's goal is only the restoration of good health. There might be different medications but there is no difference in the ideology. One medicine suiting one patient may not suit another patient who has a different physical condition. Similarly, spiritual instructions given to one aspirant may not appeal to another. The knowledge or advice given to an aspirant who has a certain background may not be suitable for who another who has a different background. There is no fault regarding the methods that Mother Shruti (the Vedas) gives. The faults are in the mental disposition of the aspirants at the time the exposition is made. Mother Shruti's final goal is to make all children attain Self-Knowledge. Therefore the aspirant should abandon the faultfinding attitude, and fulfill oneself by achieving the goal of acquiring Self-Knowledge.

Chapter 4: The Great-Causal Body - "I Am"

Up to this point in the text, the explanation has focused on the definition of the four bodies. Now we will see how "Knowledge" arises in these four bodies. To gain the knowledge of objects with sight through the Gross Body, it is necessarily implied that all of the four bodies are instrumental in bringing this about. If we take into consideration a pair of eyes that are drawn in a picture, it is obvious to us that those eyes cannot see an object. In the same way, the physical eyes alone cannot see an object without the help of the subtle eye of the intellect. For example, we see a mango, or have the knowledge that "this is a mango," but what would happen if we were only to just see what the physical eyes alone see? Of course, the physical eye should also see the object as a mango. However, it does not happen like that. Behind the physical eye is the subtle eye of the intellect whose help is sought to know the "mango."

However, even this combination of the physical eye and the subtle intellect is not sufficient. If these two do not have the support of the Causal Body, the intellect is dead. The Causal Body functions in various ways, like space, sky, the void, distance, etc. The intellect needs the background of space in order to function. So, now there is the eye, the intellect, and space in the form of the Causal Body, but if there is no witness, in the form of the Great-Causal body (Consciousness; "I Am") to connect these three, there is no knowledge of anything.

Thus, in order to get the knowledge of objects, it is necessary for all four of these bodies to be present. However, if we look progressively from one body to the next, it needs to be pointed out that in order to know the activity or changes in the Subtle Body, the Physical Body is not necessary. Additionally, the activity or changes that occur in the Subtle Body such as attraction and repulsion, thirst and hunger, and pleasure and pain, can be known only with the aid of the Causal and Great-Causal Bodies. However, looking in the other direction, in order for knowledge to arise in the Causal Body, the help of the Gross and the Subtle Bodies is not required. At this stage in the explanation, it must be made clear that knowledge on any level is always dependent on the Great-Causal Body.

For gaining knowledge in the Causal Body, the elements of the Subtle Body (mind, intellect, thinking, prana, and the senses) are of absolutely no use. The elements of the Subtle Body only have influence over the Gross and Subtle Bodies. The field of the Causal Body is entirely different from the Gross and Subtle Bodies, and nothing from them can ever step into it. The question naturally arises at this point, "If this is the case, how then, can one enter into the Great-Causal Body?" It is a fact that the scope of the mind and intellect is limited only to the Subtle Body and they do not have the capacity to enter the further two bodies, the Causal Body, and the Great-Causal Body.

At this point, it must be stated that the "Knowledge" of the Great-Causal Body (Turya) is absolutely "Self-Sufficient." It stands on its own, and has no dependency or expectation of help from the previous three bodies mentioned earlier. This Knowledge is "Self-Luminous." By way of analogy, even though the eye sees all objects, no object can see the eye. No one feels the need of the light of a lamp to see the sun. Similarly, nobody is capable of seeing this "King of Knowledge," which is the eye of the eye.

This "Knowledge" proves its own existence by its own luminosity. Even though the eye cannot see itself, anyone who has eyes never has doubts as to whether he has eyes or not. He can see because he has eyes. This type of certainty naturally abides in him. Similarly, one has knowledge of oneself while witnessing someone or something other than oneself. In order to see our eyes, we need a mirror in order to see the reflection of the eyes. That objective knowledge is only the "reflected knowledge" of the eyes. However, the "Knowledge" of the Great-Causal Body proves its own existence by witnessing everything other than itself. For its proof of existence, no other evidence is required.

This Knowledge of the Great-Causal Body is "all-pervading," and yet, it is as if it were invisible from the ignorant being's point of view. Instead of seeing the "Knowledge" of the Great-Causal Body, for him the Gross Body, which in proportion is like a poppy seed in the ocean, has become the biggest thing of all. The ways of this world are indeed perverse. It has become our habit that when looking at a smaller thing, that which is objective, we forget the bigger thing, that which is subjective. We abandon that which is "Self-Proving," and "Self-Sufficient," and praise artificial things. It is like when words of praise are given to beautiful electric lights, yet we fail to give the same praise to the light of the sun, or when we look at the pictures painted on a wall, and forget the wall itself. The process is such that even when we look at a wall, we forget the house itself, and when we discover objects in the light, we forget about the light, and when we are reading letters written on a piece of paper, we are not conscious of the paper at all.

What actually happens in this process is that in spite of the fact that the pervading substance is infinitely bigger, when we pay attention to the pervaded object we forget the pervading substance. (The examples of gold and the ornaments, or earth and the wall are commonly used to illustrate this point.) The Gross is pervaded by the Subtle, the Subtle is pervaded by the Causal, and the Causal is pervaded by the Great-Causal (Consciousness, or Knowledge). However, even with this being the case, the "Knowledge" of the Great-Causal Body cannot be seen because everyone's attention is focused on the Gross, and that which is objective. When the narrow focus of the aspirant widens, becoming that which is all-pervading, then one will have the vision of Truth, the "Infinite Knowledge" that covers and envelopes the vastness of Space.

Although the Knowledge that abides in the Great-Causal Body is the destroyer of the Causal Body (Ignorance), it cannot destroy the Gross and Subtle Bodies. The ordinary and superficial objective knowledge that is gained through the Gross and Subtle Bodies is *not* the destroyer of Ignorance. Only that extraordinary unique "Knowledge" of the Great-Causal Body is the opponent of Ignorance. Ignorance is actually sustained by ordinary objective knowledge. It is only after achieving that "Knowledge" which is "original," that Ignorance vanishes. However, at the same time, the functioning of the Gross and Subtle Bodies does not stop.

Just as the Gross and Subtle Body's inherent activities function for an ignorant man, these activities also continue to function for the Jnani after he has gained "Self-Knowledge." It is similar to the analogy of how the objects that are invisible in darkness are seen when the darkness is destroyed by the light of a lamp. The light destroys the darkness, but not the objects themselves. It is by the power of the light that the objects become known. It is only the darkness that is destroyed while the objects are illuminated. In the same way, when one gains Self-Knowledge, the darkness of Ignorance is completely eradicated, yet the Gross and Subtle Bodies continue functioning.

In the natural progression of this exposition, the question arises, "In the Light of the Knowledge of the Great-Causal Body, and with the destruction of Ignorance, will the Causal Body cease functioning? Let us give this point some thought. Ignorance has many forms such as sky, space, point of contact, distance, etc. After gaining Self-Knowledge it is true that Ignorance is destroyed. In this Self-Knowledge, all impulses or activity (movement) appear in space as either subtle or gross desires. These impulses will not arise at all unless the space is first created.

So what happens is this: When one looks at these bodies after gaining Self-Knowledge, the four bodies appear, or are viewed, in reverse order from the sequence that was used when each body was being transcended in the process of arriving at the "Knowledge of the Self." First Self-Knowledge ("I Am"), then the Causal Body in the form of space, then the Subtle Body, and after that, the Gross Body, all readily appear and take form. However, before the activities and functioning of the Gross and Subtle Bodies become apparent, although the Ignorance in the Causal Body has been destroyed, out of necessity the Causal Body establishes a "step of space" between the Subtle Body, and the Great-Causal Body.

Chapter 5: The Appearance of the World

When "Knowledge" begins to stir, activity or motion arises, and the Causal Body in the form of the space of Consciousness, or "Chidakash," is simultaneously created. Then in sequence comes the Subtle Body, and then, the Gross Body appears. In the method of gaining Self-Knowledge that has been expounded previously, the four steps that are ascended in sequence are:

1) The Gross Physical Body
2) The Subtle Body
3) The Causal Body
4) The Great-Causal Body

Now the same sequence is reversed:

1) The Great-Causal Body
2) The Causal Body
3) The Subtle Body
4) The Gross Physical Body

Instead of Knowledge abiding peacefully within itself, it begins to stir and begins its downward descent. The last two steps, those of the Subtle Body and the Gross Body, cannot be stepped upon unless the third step, the "Causal Body" is first stepped upon. Stepping down from this "Causal State," the last two steps, the Subtle and Gross Bodies arise, and it is on these steps alone that the appearance of the world is felt.

Ultimately what happens is this: The Knowledge that contains the appearance of the world has not been able to completely destroy Ignorance. Think about how light destroys darkness, thus giving us the knowledge of objects which were previously unknown because of the darkness. Similarly, the world appears only because the Causal Body has sustained it, or preserved it, in "Space." As long as the appearance of the world is felt by either the Jnani (one who has realized "I Am"), or an ignorant one, it must be understood that Ignorance is still lurking in one form or another. The difference being that Ignorance does not appear to a Jnani in that particular form (The Jnani experiences Ignorance as Knowledge). Unless Knowledge dies, Ignorance does not die. Knowledge and Ignorance are Siamese twins born of Illusion (Maya). They are both born, and both die, at the same time. If one is there, the other lives on, and when one dies the other is no more. Since this is the Truth, we will see how Knowledge itself dies. Before the Knowledge in the Great-Causal Body dies, the bodies that are below it must all die. These four bodies die in sequence. When looking at a dying man, we do nothing but look at him. We do not die with him. In the same way, we can calmly look within ourselves at how these four bodies die.

One principle that can be easily noticed about death, is that when growth stops, dissolution begins. The meaning of this statement is that whenever something stops growing, it starts disintegrating and follows the path of death. It is unnecessary to do any work for death. Destruction is inherent in growth. In birth, there is death, and in death, there is birth. This is the tradition of birth and death. An object that is born dies its own death, even though there may apparently be some other reason. The root cause of death is nothing other than birth. These four bodies have come upon the "Pure Nature" and they have to die. How do they die? We shall see. The death of the Physical Gross Body according to the principle of "where there is growth, there is destruction" can never be avoided. If not today, at least after one hundred years, or some length of time, whatever it may be. The Gross Body grows until the age of twenty-five or so, and after that, the body begins disintegrating and slowly walks along the "Highway of Death," until one day it becomes a victim of death. As the Gross Body is only the physical form of the Subtle Body, it can be said that it has no separate independent existence. A tree in its gross form is nothing but the result of its seed, which is the subtle form. Both forms of this tree automatically die off.

The Subtle Body is the seed of birth and death. This seed does not get destroyed as easily as a tree. Its growth is so enormous that if it is not sought out and destroyed by man's effort, it will keep on growing indefinitely. This growth becomes the cause of an infinite number of gross bodies. This is what puts a being through births in 8.4 million species. When the growth of the Physical Body naturally stops, the Subtle Body does not stop growing. It is here, that one feels the need for a Sadguru in order to understand how to stop the growth of the Subtle Body. Arresting the growth of the Subtle Body of imagination and doubts means giving up dreams and desires. Desires, dreams, worries, imagination, etc. are the products of the mind. The task of breaking them can be done only with one's own mind. Whatever is created by the mind cannot be destroyed by the hand, and conversely whatever is created by the hand cannot be destroyed by the mind. Whenever we try to forcefully break up these dreams and desires, their number only seems to grow. The mind is frivolously disrespectful. When we try to curb it, it becomes more agitated. Therefore, to stop the growth of the mind, the Sadguru gives us the remedy. "If you try to keep quiet, gradually the imagination and doubts dissolve." When a small infant is sleeping, if you observe its eyes for some time you can easily learn a lesson from him how to stay quiet. When going to sleep, you will see how easily the infant slips into sleep, forgetting himself. While you are looking at the baby, you can also slip into the state of forgetfulness devoid of imaginings, dreams, desires, worries, and doubts.

While a thorn can be taken out by the trick of using another thorn, the mind can only be broken with the mind. Birth and death, or appearing and disappearing, are the two opposite sides of the same state of Consciousness. When one comes, the other goes, and conversely when one goes, the other comes. Death dies its own death like the demon Bhasmasura who put his hand on his own head thereby destroying himself. Thus, when the mind is broken the state that is the Causal Body in the form of Forgetfulness gets completely exposed, and the aspirant gets the "Knowledge" of that state called "Forgetfulness." The remedy is to diligently practice remembering the instruction, or the repetition of the mantra given by the Guru. Once one begins to stop the growth of the mind, the mind slowly goes along the path of death, and can gradually be completely annihilated. Moreover, one's study and putting into practice the teaching learned from the Sadguru have to be persistent. For example, once a tree starts drying up, even if one tries to keep it green, it will in due time start breaking up, then become uprooted, and eventually fall. Even if one puts plasters on the top of it, paints it, and tries to repair it again and again, a time will come when it comes crumbling down. In the same way, if the mind is constantly stopped from growing, one day it will automatically become tired and break up. However, the aspirant should not become tired of practicing.

In this way, by persistent practice, the next body, the Causal Body, becomes exposed after the death of the Subtle Body. Once the curtain of the Subtle Body is destroyed, it ceases functioning as a covering over the Causal Body, and the Causal Body automatically becomes exposed. Now let us see how the Causal Body dies. The Causal Body is the producer, or the father, of the Subtle Body. Whenever any state comes uninvited (the Causal Body is not invited) it is experienced for a short time, and once the flood of it recedes it is not remembered. The state of it while it is coming is forceful and growing, yet once the flood ebbs away, it is not even remembered. After having submerged everything for a short period of time, it begins to dissipate, and at last it becomes as if it were not there at all and completely disappears. When a human being is getting roasted in the hot sun and then moves under the cool shade of a tree, at that very moment, the flood of cool peace comes to him with such force that he lets out "laugh" as an expression of joy. This shows that the flood of peace is overflowing from the inside as well as outside of him. However, after some time, that "laugh" automatically passes and he lies quietly unaware of his surroundings. Similarly, when the subtle qualities of the Subtle Body, such as its hurry and its struggle, becomes comparatively less, forgetfulness in the form of the peaceful void of the Causal Body is automatically forgotten. When this negative state is negated, it results only in negation. To kill it does not require a sword of a positive statement of the "I Am." Shri Samartha Ramdas made this clear by the statement, "The negative is negated by its own negation."

When the state of forgetfulness is dissolved, the Fourth Body, the state of Knowledge that is the Turya State becomes exposed automatically (Turyasvastha - consciousness of "Consciousness"). This state of Knowledge comes to a being with the help of what? It comes in relationship with the state of Ignorance. But even this state of Knowledge, although very powerful, also dissolves eventually. When one attains Knowledge, it is necessary that the Knowledge also must be dissolved. That which comes, has to go. As Ignorance comes, likewise, Knowledge comes. Thus when the Knowledge that is the Great-Causal Body dies, Parabrahman, which is inherent in all of the four bodies, is exposed. This Parabrahman, is "That" which is never born, and never ever dies. After each respective body dies, "That One" who sees the death of all of these bodies, yet remains, is your Real Nature.

Experiencing the Castes in a Human Being

Lord Krishna said in the Bhagavad Gita, "I have created four types of castes." This can be a subject of experience for any human being in his own self. "My creation is divided into four parts and these parts are divided according to their quality and Karma (activity). The four castes are Brahmana (Brahmin; Priest), Kshatriya (Warrior), Vaishya (Merchant), and Shudra (Laborer)." The four bodies can be viewed along the same lines. The Great-Causal Body is of the Brahmin Caste, the Causal Body is of the Warrior Caste, the Subtle Body is of the Merchant Caste, and the Gross Body is of the Laborer Caste. In this way, Paramatman was dispersed into these parts within Himself. The Gross Body is heavy which is an instrument used for service and labor, and therefore, it is the Shudra (laborer) Caste. Sitting on a mattress in the Gross Body, taking a balance in hand, and managing the business of the whole world, is the intellect (Buddhi) who compares things as good and bad, big and small, and employs the "laborer" (Gross Body) as a servant to gets things done as he likes, because he is the master. For this reason, this Subtle Body is the Vaishya (merchant) Caste. Now look at the brave actions of the Causal Body. The Causal Body establishes his kingdom by swallowing up the entire wealth in the form of the world that was accumulated on the strength of the capital of desires, imagination, dreams, and doubts. It also swallows up the servants in the form of the Gross and Subtle Bodies. This causality which is one of total destruction is the attitude of a warrior, and therefore the state of the Causal Body is that of the Kshatriya (warrior) Caste.

Now, what remains is only the Great-Causal Body (Brahmin caste). In this body, there is a complete neglect of all the other three bodies. "I have nothing to do with the Gross Body, which puts in hard labor and dies. Neither do I have anything to do with that merchant in the form of intellect, who trades in ideas and dreams, and spreads a big panorama of the world. I have also nothing to do with the warrior in the form of the Causal Body who sits quietly as if nothing has happened after killing both the subtle and gross bodies. They all may do nothing, or let the Gross Body groan under hard labor, and let the Subtle Body do business with the world, and let the Causal Body wage war against these two. What have I do to with any of these?" There is a saying, "Think of the Self (Rama) and let the world fight." Knowing this very well, the Great-Causal Body went on announcing the Vedic words "I am Brahman, Aham Brahmasmi," and sat quietly on his own ground, reaching the high stage of Brahmanhood. This Brahmana (Brahmin) is very orthodox about the touch of another caste and cannot tolerate the touch of another body. The other bodies hold the Great-Causal Body in high esteem and smear their heads with the dust of his feet. From the point of view of Vijnana (Supreme Knowledge, or Final Reality), even if this Great-Causal Body becomes polluted by being in contact with the other bodies, it is still the most sacred and highest in all the three worlds (the three bodies, the states of Waking, Deep Sleep, and Ignorance).

The Three Worlds

The Gross Body is the "Material World" (Swarga Loka), the Subtle Body is the "World of Birth and Death" (Mrityu Loka), and the Causal Body is the "Nether World" (Patala Loka). The Great-Causal Body is Brahman. These bodies are divided according to their qualities and these worlds are known by these qualities. The Gross Body is the Swarga Loka and sits on top of, or covers the other worlds. All sorts of external enjoyments and activities are experienced in this world. The wonderful gardens, and the beautiful forests, are created for this world only, and the presiding deity here is Brahma Deva, the Creator, whose main quality is activity, or the Rajas guna. The world below this is the world of death and birth, called Mrityu Loka. In this Loka is a big factory of birth and death where the qualities of appearing and disappearing are continuously being processed. This continuous process is nothing but the rising (birth) and setting (death) of mental modifications. In this way, one is born many times and dies many times during the same day. Everyone should keep for himself an account of his births and rebirths. Every idea produces a visible appearance, and when that idea sets, the appearance also sets. In this way when ideas stop, it is the end of and era, or Kalpanta (final dissolution of concepts). This is experienced continuously in the Subtle Body. The scriptural writers have accepted the principle of creation and appearance. They stated that as soon as an idea rises, the world rises, and when the idea sets, the world sets. Unless the Subtle Body in the form of Mrityu loka is permanently destroyed and buried, hundreds of eras are sure to rise and set. Therefore, one should die such a death that eliminates the further necessity of being born at all, and live in one's "True Nature" in such a way that there is no fear of any further experience of dying. Let this be so. Whatever has to happen will happen, but until then, it is certain that this Mrityu Loka keeps its mouth wide open for entry. The abode of the Subtle Body is the "Inner-Mind," which is known as the "Antahkarana," or "Consciousness." The presiding deity here is Vishnu, and He nourishes the world. (Note - Antahkarana is a word that has no English equivalent, and is difficult to define. Shri Siddharameshwar used this word frequently in many of his talks, so it warrants some basic explanation. It is generally considered to be the "Seat of Consciousness" that is the "spark" or genesis of subtle manifestation arising out of "Formless Existence." It is characterized by the motion of the attributes arising out of the objectless Consciousness. One could say it is the source of the mind, or one's innermost mind, or innermost heart. It is the origination of, or assertion of, objectivity. It is the mind at its most subtle. Shri Siddharameshwar Maharaj has said about it, "The Inner-Mind of all is the same, while their minds are different." Throughout this text it is translated as "Inner-Mind" for consistency)

The world below that Knowledge of the Inner-Mind is Patala Loka (The Nether World), which is the Causal Body in the form of forgetfulness. In Patala Loka, there is the pitch darkness of Ignorance. The destroyer, "Rudra" (Shiva) who is of the quality of Ignorance, or Tamas, is the presiding deity here. Above these three is the Great-Causal Body, which is the highest body and is therefore higher than these three worlds. The presiding deity here is "Pure Knowledge." That Knowledge rules here and is the God of all gods. From this God, all the worlds are produced, and He is called "The Lord of the three worlds," (Trailokyanath). The Brahmana (Brahmin) is the Guru of all the castes (Varanas) and therefore is placed most highly among them. This gives him the status of a Master. This Brahmana does not allow even the shadow of Ignorance to fall on Him. What's more is that he refuses to even become polluted by the mind and intellect. So, give up the idea that He will ever embrace the corpse of the Gross Body. This orthodox clean Brahmin in the form of "Pure Consciousness," or "Universal

Cosmic Consciousness" does not allow even a single entrant into His Great-Causal Body. Therefore, it should be understood that none of these bodies, or castes (Warrior/Causal Body; Trader/Subtle Body; Laborer/Gross Body), can ever enter into His abode. This means that the Gross and Subtle Bodies can never enter the Great-Causal Body. These bodies (castes) cannot do anything without the help of this Brahmana, the Primal Knowledge "I Am." All of their good and bad actions or works only go on the support and strength of this Brahmana. At this time, the Brahmana comes out of his dwelling and accomplishes the work of these three castes. As soon as the work is done, he cleans himself of any traces of them right in front of their doorstep, and only then enters back into His "Own Abode."

Understanding the Knowledge of Self

Brahman is rich with Knowledge. That is why he is called Vedo Narayana (Knowledge that is God residing in All). He knows all the three times (the beginning, the middle, and the end), and He has a characteristic of Sandhya, which is the space between any two thoughts. He is worshipped by all people and therefore is also called the Lord of Earth. The people of all castes and creeds worship this God whether they are aware of it or not. The worshipper may be a Hindu, a Muslim, a Christian, a Jain, a Parsee, or a Buddhist. He may be from any country such as Iran, Turkey, etc., yet he only worships this One God, whoever he may be. He cannot help it. When this God is hungry, all types of food and drink are offered to Him. There are mattresses with cushions made into beds ready for Him to sleep upon. If He feels like traveling, there are cars, airplanes, and many other types of transportation ready for him. To supply Him with fragrant garlands, there are many trees and vines that blossom forth laden with flowers. All servants and attendants are ready to obey Him with folded hands. The wife, children, and palaces, are for His entertainment, and they are also His dwelling place. God is dwelling in the innermost heart of all beings, and receiving all of the different kinds of service that are rendered unto Himself. Yet, in spite of His greatness and omnipresence, we consider the body as God, and offer all kinds of services to it. The ignorant people have accepted this wrong idea, and have misunderstood the whole affair. It is this idea that has separated God from His devotee. What is there to be amazed about?

Those who are doing any actions are doing it for no other reason than out of worship rendered to Him. This Great God (Mahadeva) is constantly enjoying the shower of all the objects of the senses in the form of sound, forms, touch, taste, and smell. He receives everything that is of the nature the five instruments of senses of action and the five instruments of knowledge. That devotee is indeed glorious who understands the secret of this Great God, Mahadeva. All natural acts of such a devotee are dedicated to Brahman. The bees, birds, insects, and even the ants, are performing worship to this God. However, they don't have the intellect to understand this so they cannot be blamed for their ignorance. However, it is unfortunate indeed that the intelligent human being does not understand that all of his daily and occasional actions, are but for the sake of this One God, alone. How very unfortunate this is.

This God is the same as the "King of Knowledge" who while swallowing a mouthful of food, tastes and enjoys it. It is He, who discriminates between fragrance and stench. It is He, who understands which sound is pleasant to the ear, and which sound is harsh. It is He, who observes the difference between a beautiful, or a fierce and ugly form. It is He who understands the soft or hard touch. He is always present, reigning supreme in every being's heart. How utterly misguided is the idea that we worship any other God than this One. Just think of which God is worshipped when the Christians worship Christ, the Hindus worship Vishnu or Shiva, the Parsees worship their Zoroaster, or the Buddhists their Buddha? Are they not merely worshipping the corpses of these mentioned Gods? However, what is the feeling of the devotee who is worshipping? Ask anyone from any religion "Describe your

God," and they will answer "My God is Conscious, Luminous, Solid, Omniscient, Omnipresent, and Omnipotent. He animates all, and owns all. He is without birth, and without death." Will anyone say that his God is a stone, or a rock, or mud, or metal, or heavy, dull, and vacant without Consciousness, or that he is weak, blind, or deaf?

From this, it is clear that whether it is Christ, Vishnu, Buddha, Zoroaster, or whatever God it may be, His nature will be full of Consciousness, and He is full of the "Qualities of God." If anyone possesses all of these qualities, then the indication is that He is the Absolute Paramatman. He is God in the form of "Knowledge" that is present in everyone's heart. This God alone dwelled in Mohammed, and Christ's heart was pervaded by this One God as well. It is only by this God that the quality of Vishnu (The Protector) has been sustained, and not by any other God. For any devotee whomever he may be that worships any God, that worship is the worship of this "One Inner Self." The obeisance made to any other Gods, go to this One God, (Our Own Self Nature), alone. This is the "Absolute Truth."

The forms of all the above-mentioned Gods, are only temples of this "One God." All the names belong to His temples (bodies). He is present in the innermost region, of all these forms. He sits in all of the forms of all beings and accepts all of their worship. Whatever actions are done by the Gross Body, and whatever imagination or desires, or concepts and doubts that have crossed the mind happen for the sake of this God, in order to please Him. If you recognize this much, your work is done. All of you are doing something through your body or mind. If you say, "We do not want to do it," you cannot stop from doing it. However, whatever you do, the doer, and enjoyer of your deeds is only God (The Self). This fact alone must be recognized in every movement. All auspicious and inauspicious acts thus become dedicated to Brahman, and the aspirant remains absolutely free. This is what is called the "Sacrifice through Knowledge" (Jnana Yadnya).

When you come and go, speak or swallow, when you give or take, stand or sit, do any action at home or outside, or are in bed enjoying sex, leave off all sense of shame or doership, and think only of God. It is the "One Knowledge" alone is playing at each point. To contemplate on this, means contemplating on God. The body-consciousness has to be turned into Self-Consciousness. The decision that the Self alone is doing all, is itself the state of Liberation. This is the advice given by Samartha Ramdas. Even Saint Tukaram asked for this gift from God. "May I never, never, forget you." Likewise, we also must never forget the Self. Then surely salvation is at your feet. As this rope, in the form of the mind, was twisted in the direction of body-consciousness, it now has to be twisted in the opposite direction of Self-Consciousness. When the rope gets untwisted, the strings will be blown about in the wind, and there will be nothing left to call "rope."

When a screw is screwed in, it has to be turned in the opposite direction to come out. Similarly, with regard to body-consciousness, if the mind which is guided by the intellect is directed towards the Self, it becomes absorbed in the Self. As the mind is directed towards the One God, Lord Rama, it gets absorbed in Rama. The mind itself becomes Rama, and there is nothing left in the form of the mind, inside or out, or anywhere, and it becomes one with the form of Rama. Take this advice, and you will see this for yourself. To better understand just how the "One Pure Knowledge" is playing about, you have only to come out of the house, and look at the moon. With what speed does the Pure Consciousness rush towards the moon out from the window of your mind? See how it pervades the whole sky in a fraction of a second. Try this.

Does the mind have this much speed? The mind received the speed of awareness of the moon, only through the help of this "Knowledge." Wherever the mind goes, Consciousness is already there. What a wonder it is then that the movement of the mind seems stuck in this Consciousness. You only have to open the eyelids, and the "Knowledge" (Consciousness) simultaneously pervades the entire sky, the vastness that contains the multitude of stars, and the moon. Instead of saying that it pervades, it is better to say that it has already pervaded the whole, which is now experienced.

When Consciousness travels from the eye to the moon and one recognizes it to be the moon, this is the objective knowledge. In this example, the moon is the object, and the Consciousness takes its shape immediately upon knowing that it is the moon. If there is a cloud in front of the moon, the Consciousness takes the shape of the cloud, and is viewed as that object. Thus, Consciousness pervades the cloud and knows the cloud to be an object.

Chapter 6: Maya and Brahman

Now, try to notice the "crust" of Consciousness without an object, the "Pure Knowledge" without the mixture of any objects. That space, which is lying between the eye and the moon, did not come to your notice, yet still it was there pervading, existing in its own nature. That is the pure form of Knowledge. When empty space that is not noticed previously, is purposefully made an object of attention, it becomes the object of attention, as "Space." What can be noticed is Maya, and whatever cannot be seen is "Brahman." While looking at the moon, the space in between did not come to your attention. Therefore, it is Consciousness without an object. If this space is separated, and is made an object of sight this Pure Knowledge is transformed into a zero, because if space is seen separately, the modification of the mind becomes a void. If there is any difference between Space, and Pure Knowledge it is this: To separately look at one's own nature is Space, and when the "looking" is abandoned, it is "Pure Knowledge." Once Pure Knowledge is recognized properly in this manner, even when mixed with any object, it can be selected and recognized. Once pure water is known, even when it is mixed with something else, its existence can be recognized within that mixture. Water is a fluid that can become condensed into ice. Even when water gives up its fluidity and assumes the density of ice, it is still recognized as water in the form of ice. It is not difficult to recognize the wetness in mud as water. Similarly, once Pure Knowledge is known, its steady existence in this moving world in the form of Sat-Chit-Ananda (Being, Consciousness, and Bliss) can also be recognized.

Pure water is devoid of any color, form, taste, or smell. Once this is properly understood, even when water is condensed to assume a dense form, or takes on a hot flavor by adding chilies, or a sweet flavor by adding sugar, or if it becomes fragrant, or takes on a color such as rose, or is used as water in paint, it is quite unmistakably still recognized as pure water, or water minus the form, the taste, the smell, and the color. Thus, by the same method of elimination, even when this Pure Knowledge is conditioned, by subtracting the conditioning and by dividing the form into its respective elements, it will be recognized as absolutely Pure Knowledge alone that fills every form everywhere, to the brim. However, before attaining this Pure Knowledge by the method of elimination, if someone accepts the method of enumeration (listing the qualities of God), and goes on chattering about how God alone pervades all beings, and all forms, and that there is nothing else but Rama, and that "the world, and the Lord of the world, are but one," etc., etc., then such babble can never be useful. In contrast to this type of chatter, if one speaks only empty words without having the experience behind them, such as, "I am Brahman," or "the senses do their job, yet I am not the doer," or "there is no sin or virtue at my doorstep," etc., instead of gaining the Self, he will only deceive the Self. In this way, these so-called "Self-discoverers" lose the joy of this world, as well as that of the other world. Saint Kabir said; "He went away as he came." This means that these people die in the same state of consciousness as that in which they were born. They get no benefit from life other than this.

Such worldly scholars take words to be true Self-Knowledge, but has that Truth which is beyond speech ever dawned on an ignorant man? Anyone can say "The senses do the work of the senses, but I am not the senses," or "The mind's qualities are with the mind, and body's qualities are with the body, but what have I to do with them? I am different from these." What is untrue about these utterances? Who is it that understands the Truth? Who is it that has the experience of Truth? Only the one who knows who he is. Of what use are such statements to another? Each one enjoys his own pleasures and bliss. Tukaram said "Each one for himself." Even a parrot can be taught to repeatedly say the words "Brahman is Truth, the world is only an appearance." However, one cannot say that the parrot has understood the Truth of what Brahman is, or what the world is, or even what a statement of Truth is. Where there is no understanding there cannot be the "Bliss of Self-Knowledge."

Let that be as it is. However, an aspirant should not follow the example of one who is an expert with words, yet is a hypocrite. With persistent study, and by applying the method of elimination, one must first come to know what Pure Knowledge is. Knowledge is of different types, such as general, particular, objective knowledge of imagination and doubts, and the Knowledge that is without any thought. The particular, objective, imagining, and doubting types of knowledge are contradictory to Pure Knowledge. When the Pure Consciousness through process of sight takes the shape of an object, one gets objective knowledge, or knowledge which can be of a particular type, or an imagination type, or of a doubt type of knowledge. If the object is gross, it is objective knowledge. If it is only an idea that is subtle, it is idea knowledge, or Savikalpa. This means that when Pure Knowledge takes the shape of an object, an idea, or a thought, it then becomes categorized as particular knowledge. Particular knowledge, being artificial, is by nature transient and lasts only for a very short period of time. It is inherently transient and of an unsteady nature. However, the rule is that particular knowledge must return back into general knowledge, the knowledge that "I Am."

As an example, when we walk, this is considered the common or general speed, and when we increase the speed and start running, it becomes a particular speed. Yet, how long can we run? After sometime the running stops, and soon one assumes the natural speed again. Similar to this, we are naturally very loving and blissful within, and this love within oneself is the general type of love common to all. However, when love is for a son, a friend, or a house, etc., it is an objective and a particular kind of love. Thus, a love that comes, must also go. The love that comes, is of a particular kind which is transient and destructible. The happiness that one gets from objects, also falls into the category of being of a "particular" kind of happiness which only lasts for a very short period of time. A small thing brings in an experience of "particular" type, but while our attention is focused on that, the "One Thing" that pervades it cannot be experienced. The reason is, is that the pervading thing is big and infinite, and in reality we are that same "All-Pervading Brahman." The "particular" thing is Maya, and the general or common thing is Brahman, and we are "That." When we are focused on the experience of a "particular type" we do not experience "The Love of Our Own Self," nor do we enjoy "The Happiness of the Bliss of the Self."

We will now observe what is called "general knowledge" which is devoid of an object or an idea. There is a slight distance between an outside gross object and the eye, or the mind. That void or space although unknowingly observed, is as if it were not seen, and therefore we have no knowledge or acknowledgment of that space. This intervening knowledge (the space) being "Knowledge" itself, cannot become the object of its own knowledge. How can sugar taste its own sweetness? In the same way, Knowledge does not experience itself as an object. This Knowledge is naturally spread out between the eye and the object, as well as between the intellect and an idea or thought. One should repeatedly take notice of how this general "Pure Knowledge" naturally pervades everywhere before it acknowledges or recognizes an object. This noticing, or "seeing," is not the same as seeing an object such as, "I am the seer of an object," or "I am the thinker, of an idea." It is only seen when one gives up both the seeing as well as the thought that "I am the seer." The instrument of seeing is the eye, and the instrument of knowing a thought is the intellect. "Knowledge" itself can only be seen by setting aside both of these instruments. The instruments of sight and the intellect are of no value here. Any attempt to know Pure Knowledge by means of the eye or intellect is to forget that Pure Knowledge (the unadulterated sense of "I Am) by allowing these instruments to step in. To know Pure Knowledge really means not to know it, and once "known" in this way, the "knower" himself becomes Pure Knowledge.

Samartha Ramdas has said "In trying to meet Pure Knowledge one becomes separated from it. But there is always union with it without trying to meet it." This puzzle is very difficult. Wise men, yogis, and renunciates make a mistake and misinterpret the seen, as the seer, when saying "Paramatman is like 'this.' He has four hands. He is like the light of a million suns. He is lustrous. He is dark complexioned. He is like a point, and He is like this and He is like that." etc. They say whatever they like, but by whose knowledge is it that it is stated that "This one is like this, and the other is like that"? "That One" is forgotten completely while they talk of the great things of Realization. However, when the seer is forgotten whatever is seen is "I," which is Brahman. One does not know what to say of this. The brave one sets out to find Brahman but the obstacle in the form of the seen gets in his way. This is the state of the majority of seekers.

Search for the Lost "I"

In a crowd during a pilgrimage, I lost myself and could not find myself even when I tried searching within. Then, I went to the police station and gave them the information that I was lost. At that time a constable came and slapped my cheeks hard until they were red and asked me, "Who is this fellow?" Only then did I become conscious of myself, and was very happy that I was found. This is the very condition of the one that is himself Brahman and yet is in search of Brahman. Where and how can He find Himself? His exact position is such that He is the one who knows everyone but is not known by anyone. The one who tries to know Him does not know that his own true nature is "Pure Consciousness" so he wanders about in the forest and jungle (searching for that which has never been lost). How amazing this is! How can He, the one who is known only after "the capacity of knowing" has been transcended, be known? Unless one becomes steady within oneself, leaving behind having the desire to know, one cannot have the "Knowledge of Brahman.

There is a story of one foolish fellow who wanted to know what sleep was. Whenever he would start to doze off, he immediately would remember "Aha, now I will catch sleep." With that thought, he would clap his hands and suddenly become completely awake. Repeatedly doing this, the poor fellow became tired and entirely gave up his efforts of trying to catch sleep. Similarly, trying to know Brahman is the same thing. When one gives up trying to "know" Brahman, one becomes Brahman Itself. When the Gross and Subtle Bodies are negated the instruments of the mind and intellect are broken up. The aspirant then goes to the state of the Causal Body which is the state of "Forgetfulness." This itself is the Ignorance of the human being. To eradicate this Ignorance, it is necessary to acquire the "Knowledge of Brahman." Therefore, the aspirant tries to get the Knowledge of Brahman with the help of the subtle intellect, and that part of Consciousness that is "Pure Knowledge." Saint Shankaracharya (Shri Shankara) has called such a man a great fool. If one tries to know Brahman in this manner with the subtle intellect the Subtle Body will only go on increasing.

When the Subtle Body gets destroyed and one comes to the Causal Body, the one who is trying to know Brahman with the subtle intellect does not become steadied in the Causal Body. Instead he gets pushed back to the Subtle Body with force from the Causal Body and once again comes under the sway of imaginings, concepts, desires, and doubts. If an aspirant dreams, employing the use of words or the mind, he will never progress to where speech and mind cannot enter. Instead, he will go to a lower plane. The aspirant cannot remain as an aspirant, but has to become "One who is Realized" (a Siddha). For this, one has to cross over the steps of all of the four bodies. By constant study, one has to enter on the platforms of the four bodies, and clean and clarify them through thorough investigation and deduction. Only then can "The Truth of the Self" be invoked and become fully established. Once this is done, it is certain that the aspirant will become a Siddha.

Up to this point in the text, the exposition regarding the four bodies and the method of study has been explained. The aspirants must also have understood what has been presented. By way of analogy, if a wooden stool with four legs made in the form of the bodies has been constructed, it still is very crude. In order to make it shine properly, more effort has to be made. It is necessary to polish it in order to make it shine so that it can throw off its own light. The procedure for making something is quite different from the procedure of scrubbing and cleaning thereby making it absolutely smooth and appealing. Unless it has been manufactured in that finished condition, it will be not considered finished, nor will it return a fair price. Therefore, before becoming a Siddha, we must be aspirants for some time, persistently polishing the "Pure Knowledge" of the Great-Causal Body. It must be made completely clean.

Chapter 7: Devotion and Devotion After Liberation

We know that the Pure Knowledge in the form of Paramatman pervades every form. After knowing the Self intellectually, the best way of studying it and realizing it fully is to try to make everyone happy. It is with this practice alone that the Self is seen to be pervading in everything. The whole world is only "Knowledge." Since everything is the Self, by making everyone happy the Self is pleased. In this way, the Truth of the Vedas will be proven and experienced, and Self-Knowledge will become firmly established. The worship of Paramatman with form (Saguna) is the worship of the manifest. Brahmananda (The Bliss of Brahman) manifests in all forms such as that of an insect, ant, dog, or pig. It is the "Supreme Self," Paramatman alone, that pervades everything. Paramatman, that is formless, without any attributes and not manifest, has become manifest with qualities in the form of the Universe. He is present in those things that are inert, but is experienced clearly in all moving beings. Instead of worshipping lifeless gross objects such as stone and metal idols, it is better to worship the moving, walking, talking God in whom the quality of "Knowledge" is clearly experienced. This is Saguna worship, or worship of the manifest God. What are the qualities in a stone idol? Out of the three qualities, Sattva, Rajas, and Tamas, none of these qualities is found in inert inanimate idols made of stone or metal. However, there is one or more of these qualities found in those manifestations of God who are moving. Therefore, all beings are forms of God.

If one prays sincerely to the Saints or to a good man who is full of Sattva Guna (Knowledge and an inclination towards spiritual understanding), he becomes pleased and grants us our wishes. Yet, if we censure his Tamo Guna, he slaps our face and gives us an experience of a jolt. Therefore, worship the God who is walking and talking. For gaining knowledge, a stone is of no use. Saint Kabir gave this warning in clear words. He advised all to worship a walking talking God, alone. As soon as the word "worship" is uttered, sandalwood paste, incense, flowers, kumkum, and other various articles of worship come to mind. However, to really worship God means to please and make every being happy. Although Paramatman is "One," existing everywhere, the methods used by devotees to worship Him are different according to their conditioning and how they conceive of Him. A donkey also has God in it, yet if you fold your hands before it in obeisance, it would be like a joke or mischief played on Paramatman. Does it get pleased if you fold your hands before him? If not, then according to what is said above about worship, the worship that is pleasing to another form of God, would not really be the appropriate worship of the donkey. If the donkey were given green grass and clean water to drink, that would be proper worship to God in the form of the donkey. However, worshipping the God who has taken a human form is not just offering it food with the hands, but by pleasing him in a manner that suits him. This would be the proper worship of Paramatman. By giving someone whatever he wants, his heart is pleased, and he feels blessed.

The snake and a scorpion are also forms of God (Narayana), but to worship them consists of making obeisance to them from a distance. This means that they should be left alone to live their own lives. Instead of doing this, if you start embracing them out of devotion, that serpent God will bite you and prove to you that embracing him is not worshipping him. Here someone may raise a doubt, "How could allowing the snake and scorpion to escape alive mean that you are worshipping them? Those beings are wicked and they must be killed." I would say to them that snakes or scorpions do not bite unnecessarily unless they are touched or hurt. However, man is always ready to kill them even if they are off at a considerable distance. Is not the nature of man more wicked than the nature of a snake or a scorpion? Yes, it is, because man has the desire to kill them needlessly. Let the feeling of "The snake and scorpion are of my own nature" be firm, and then see the miracle that happens. The "Self" of a snake or a scorpion is not a stone. When your understanding becomes firm that your Self is the same as the Self in a snake or a scorpion, you will see the Self of the snake is truly one with your own Self, and there will arise no desire in the snake or scorpion to bite you. If one sees a snake as a snake, it also sees an embodied man as an enemy. You will see the same facial expression in the mirror as you have on your face. If you see a bad expression in the reflection in the mirror, is it the fault of the mirror? If you make a smiling face and look in the mirror, you do not need to order the mirror to make a smiling face. Why does the thief rob our house? It is because we also have a continuous desire to rob people in many ways and fill our house. As we develop the feeling of complete renunciation, then that feeling will be reflected in whatever comes before us. Even if you refuse to ask for anything, people are prepared to give up heaps of whatever they have for you. But the one who begs for it, does not get it.

From this discussion, a reader may get confused and say, "Maharaj your way of thinking does not seem right. To leave a snake alone after sighting it, or to accept as God the one who pickpockets a bundle of notes and do nothing is something we can never do." Agreed! I would say agreed, a hundred times! Oh aspirant, this cannot be possible because of the habit of many, many, births. This type of worship cannot be achieved all at once. Yet, a beginning can be made in small steps, for example, from the small bugs in the house, instead of the scorpions and snakes. From a petty action like not killing the bugs in the house, one should study the "Oneness of All." See the "Oneness of the Self" in every thing, and every being, and then see what a wondrous experience that you will get. You will then come to have the feeling of the Oneness in all beings, even with those who are more troublesome than the bugs, and gradually "Self-Confidence" and "Self-Experience" increase. This means that one should not proceed with the feeling, "Bugs should not be killed, they should be left alone," but instead the feeling should be that "They are of my own nature, and they are my own forms. Their happiness is my happiness." A mother experiences the feeling of joy by pleasing her child when it suckles at her breast. With that same attitude, one should experience the feeling of satisfaction by allowing the bugs to suck the blood from one's own body. This idea may be difficult to accept, but it is the beginning, or the first lesson on feeling Oneness with all beings.

Gradually and persistently studying this, the earth will be without an enemy, and fearlessness will come your way. In this way, you shall be free from all fear. When an aspirant is free from all doubts and achieves "The Knowledge of the Self," he becomes free. Although this is true, he still cannot experience "The Full Glory of Real Liberation." For example, the achieving of wealth is one thing, while the enjoying of the status after becoming wealthy, is quite another thing. In the same way, unless a feeling of "The Oneness with All" comes to the Jnani, his Self-Knowledge does not develop or spread. He is like a stingy rich man with his wealth, and he cannot get the "Complete Bliss of Liberation" while alive. Even if one achieves Self-Knowledge, unless he experiences a feeling of "Oneness with All," fearlessness does not come his way. "Full Bliss" is Fearlessness. Fear is an indication of duality. Fear is a very great impediment in the way of "Bliss arising out of Liberation." After achieving Self-Knowledge, the aspirant should worship Paramatman in the method explained previously. In this manner, dry Self-Knowledge will be moistened with Devotion. A jalebi, which is a kind of sweet that has been fried in ghee, becomes juicy and sweet only after it is fried and then put into syrup. In the same way, the Jnani gets the "Fullness of Life" through "Devotion after Self-Knowledge."

In the game called "Surfati" a player slides first from the lower to the higher house, and then brings back home all that he gets from the other houses. Only then is the game over. By gaining the knowledge all the way from the Gross to the Great-Causal Body, one has to bring this gift of Self-Knowledge back to the lower body in the same way. The factual experience that "The world is nothing but Knowledge," is itself Knowledge becoming the "Final Reality" (Vijnana). It is because of the feeling that there is someone else in the world who is not "I," that we go around night and day with a feeling of anxiety that we should protect our wife, our wealth, and our belongings from the clutches of someone else. In this way, we turn into a "Gasti" or watchman due to the feeling of possessiveness and ownership. However, when one realizes a feeling of "Oneness with Everyone," and the feeling that "I am present everywhere, I am pervading everything." On that day, the "Gasti" becomes "Agasti," the sage who drank the ocean in one sip. This ocean, which is the five elements that make up the entire universe, may not even be enough for one sip.

This is the way in which the devotee who knows the Self becomes fearless while in the body, and enjoys the "Full Celebration" of what is called "Liberation." Now, at this point, we have given the exposition about Self-Knowledge and the "Devotion after Self-Knowledge." We have reached a stage where an aspirant has become the "Self-Knowing Jnani." The end of all of the Knowledge of the Great-Causal Body bears fruit in the seeing of the whole world as oneself. This being true, Saint Ramdas still has called this Knowledge of the Great-Causal Body as being unsteady Brahman when compared with that of Paramatman (that is Parabrahman). Parabrahman is steady. It is different from the "Manifest Brahman" (Saguna Brahman), and the "Invisible Brahman" (Nirguna Brahman) associated with the four bodies, and therefore it is "No-Knowledge." So finally the Vedas have said, "Neti, Neti," meaning "not this, not this." "Not this" means it is neither Knowledge nor Ignorance. Unmoving Paramatman is the "Only Truth," it is "The Essence." "It is the root of all that is transient, and thereby without substance." Saint Samartha Ramdas has expounded upon this conclusion very nicely in *Dasbodh*.

Why is this Knowledge unsteady? Because it is given many names and attributes of masculine, feminine, and neuter gender. It is called Satchitananda, Ishwara, Ahamkara, Shesha, Narayana, the Primordial Being, and Shiva, etc. These are some of the masculine names. It is called Shakti, Prakriti, Shruti, Shambhavi, Chitkakla, Narayani, etc., and these are some of the feminine names. It is called Nija Rupam (one's own nature), the Great-Causal Body, Pure

Knowledge, Brahman, the Empire of Bliss (Anandayatnam), etc., and these names of the neuter gender. These neuter gender names have come to be known as this "Self-Knowledge." The One who is not any of these, is the Steady, the Immovable, the Essence, the "Real Brahman." The great quality of "The Knowledge of the Great-Causal Body" is much greater in comparison than the Knowledge in the Gross Body, and by the process of elimination it can be gleaned, and after having been deduced, it can once again be mixed with (as it is all-permeating). However, it cannot be interpreted that the aspirant has achieved the Parabrahman stage by virtue of expertise with the process of elimination, and once again is consciously permeating everything.

Parabrahman is "That" from where no one can return. Knowledge has been labeled as "Knowledge," but Brahman really has no name. In the Knowledge of "I Am," there is the mixture of activity or changes in the form of the world. As the mind, called "chitta," undergoes this modification, Knowledge also undergoes modification. Modifications (changes) are a state, or stage. Parabrahman is beyond all modifications. Thus, there is as much difference between "Self-Knowledge," or "I Am" (Jnana), and the Absolute (Vijnana, Parabrahman), as there is a difference between darkness and light. "Where there is a contact between the steady and the unsteady, the intellect is confused," says Shri Samartha Ramdas. According to this statement, the last misunderstanding comes in here. (Contact between the steady and unsteady indicates the presence of a very subtle duality still intact.)

Before the Knowledge ("I Am") dawns, "Forgetfulness" is misunderstood as Knowledge. In the same way, when Jnana, or Knowledge, is under-developed it is misunderstood as Vijnana which is the last stage of the "Absence of modifications" of Parabrahman. When the aspirant mistakes Self-Knowledge, or "I Am" (Jnana) for Vijnana, his progress is arrested there. Samartha Ramdas has compared this type of an undeveloped Jnani to a man who is awakened in a dream, and thinks he is awake. Yet, he is still snoring! "You think that this is wakefulness, but your Illusion has not gone," is the warning given by Shri Samartha to this type of Jnani. That Great-Causal Body, or Turya state in which the Gross and Subtle Bodies are like a dream, is itself like a dream in Vijnana. There is bondage in Ignorance, and liberation in Knowledge, but when both Ignorance and Knowledge are not there, how could the idea of bondage or liberation exist?

The Vedas and scriptures talk up to the point of the Great-Causal Body. Until then, it is the primary premise, or the theory. In the field of Knowledge beyond the Great-Causal Body is the proven final conclusion, or Siddhanta, and the canceling of all that has been laid down is right there. When all phenomena is destroyed, or annihilated, whatever remains is your "Real Nature." It is impossible to describe it in words. Where "the knowledge of words" proves to be Ignorance, where Consciousness becomes non-Consciousness, and where all remedies recommended by the scriptures are only hindrances, you will see for yourself how you reach that highest point. The Sadguru brought you to the threshold and pushed you inside, but the Sadguru cannot show you the beauty, or the panorama within. You have to seize the treasure, the trophy, yourself. Now, after all this has been said, there remains nothing that can be conveyed through words. Words were used for whatever had to be told. That which cannot be conveyed by words has now been entrusted to you. We can only inspire you to be an aspirant, but you have to become a Siddha by yourself. We have reached the end of the book. Words are redundant. One thing is clearly enunciated here, and that is Sadguru Bhajana (All Praises to the Sadguru).

Hari Om Tat Sat.

The End of Master Key to Self-Realization

www.ingramcontent.com/pod-product-compliance
Lightning Source LLC
Chambersburg PA
CBHW031128080526
44587CB00011B/1151